Jean-Baptiste Louvet de Couvray

Love and Patriotism!

Or, the extraordinary adventures of M. Duportail: late Major-general in the armies of the United States; interspersed with many surprising incidents in the life of the late Count Pulauski

Jean-Baptiste Louvet de Couvray

Love and Patriotism!

Or, the extraordinary adventures of M. Duportail: late Major-general in the armies of the United States; interspersed with many surprising incidents in the life of the late Count Pulauski

ISBN/EAN: 9783337309404

Printed in Europe, USA, Canada, Australia, Japan

Cover: Foto ©ninafisch / pixelio.de

More available books at **www.hansebooks.com**

Love and Patriotism!

OR,

THE EXTRAORDINARY ADVENTURES

OF

M. DUPORTAIL,

LATE MAJOR-GENERAL IN THE ARMIES OF THE UNITED STATES.

INTERSPERSED WITH MANY

SURPRISING INCIDENTS

IN THE LIFE OF THE LATE

COUNT PULAUSKI.

PHILADELPHIA:
PRINTED BY CAREY & MARKLAND.

1797.

Love and Patriotism!

OR,

THE EXTRAORDINARY ADVENTURES.

OF

M. DUPORTAIL,* &c.

FROM a very singular publication, which few of our readers will have an opportunity of seeing, we give the following story. It will be necessary to preface it by narrating a few particulars which are intimately connected with the history.

It was in the year 1783 that the baron de Faublas arrived in Paris, where he had resolved to place his daughter in a convent. He was accompanied by his son the chevalier de Faublas. After remaining some weeks in the capital, the baron, by the persuasion of his intimate friend, M. Duportail, came to the resolution of residing some years in Paris, for the purpose of giving the best education to the only heir of his name, and of superintending the happiness of a daughter whom he loved. The young chevalier was soon initiated into all the fashionable dissipation of the metropolis; his accomplishments were the admiration of the other sex, and the envy of his own. But while indulging in these criminal pursuits, a passion of a purer kind possessed the empire of his heart. In the course of his visits to the convent, he had seen and loved mademoiselle Sophia de Pontis, the amiable friend of his sister. The heart of Sophia yielded to the attractions of the chevalier; their passions was reciprocal. The baron was not long ignorant of their attachment; his son's visits to the convent were prohibited, and he was given to understand, that the daughter of M. Duportail was destined for his wife. What little he knew of this lady he had learned from having overheard a conversation between M. Duportail and his father, from which it appeared, that the former had long mourned a lost daughter. He farther understood, that as soon as his education was completed at Paris, it was his father's intention that he should set out on his travels; that he was to remain for some months in Poland, and that during his residence in that country, he was to be employed in making enquiry respecting the fate of the daughter of M. Duportail, and if she yet lived, in endeavouring to restore her to her afflicted father. An opportunity was soon after embraced by M. Duportail of communicating to the chevalier the particulars of his ſtory, which we now preſent to our readers.

****

My hiſtory preſents a frightful example of the inſtability of fortune. It is indeed very flattering, but it is alſo ſometimes very dangerous, to have an ancient title to ſuſtain and a large eſtate to preſerve. The ſole deſcendant of an illuſtrious family, whoſe origin is loſt in the darkneſs of remote ages, I have a right to aſpire to, and to occupy the firſt employments in the republic which gave me birth, and yet I behold myſelf condemned to languiſh in a foreign country, amidſt an indolent and inglorious obſcurity.

The name of Lovzinſki is honourably mentioned in the annals of Poland, and that name is about to periſh with myſelf. I know that an auſtere philoſophy either rejects or deſpiſes vain titles and corrupting riches, and perhaps I ſhould conſole myſelf if I had loſt only theſe; but, my young friend, I weep for an adored ſpouſe, I ſearch after a beloved daughter, and I ſhall never more re-viſit my native land. What courage is capable of oppoſing griefs like mine?

My father, the baron de Lovzinſki, ſtill more diſtinguiſhed by his virtues than by his rank, enjoyed that conſideration at court, which the favour of the prince always confers, and which personal merit sometimes obtains. He bestowed all the attention of a tender parent on the education of my two sisters; and in regard to mine, he occupied himself with the zeal of a man of family, jealous of the honour of his house, of which I was the sole hope, and with the activity of a good citizen, who desires nothing so ardently as to leave to the state a successor worthy of him.

While I was pursuing my studies at Warsaw, the young P⸺* distinguished himself among the rest of my companions by the most amiable qualities. To the charms of a person at once noble and engaging, he joined the graces of a cultivated understanding. The uncommon address which he displayed among us young warriors; that rare modesty with which he seemed desirous to conceal his own merit from himself, on purpose to exalt the abilities of his less fortunate rivals, who were generally vanquished by him in all our exercises; the urbanity of his manners, and the sweetness of his disposition, fixed the attention, commanded the esteem, and rendered him the darling of that

* The Translator thinks that he can venture to pronounce M. de P⸺ to be the nobleman who was formerly called Count Poniatowski, and who lately so worthily filled the throne of Poland.

illustrious band of young nobility, who partook of our studies and our pleasures.

To say that it was the resemblance of our characters, and the sympathy of our dispositions that occasioned my attachment to M. de P. would be to pay myself too flattering a compliment; however that may be, we both lived together in the most intimate familiarity.

How happy, but how fleeting is that time of life, when one is unacquainted with ambition, which sacrifices every thing to the desire of fortune, and the glory that follows in her train, and with love, the supreme power of which absorbs and concentres all our faculties upon one sole object! that age of innocent pleasures, and of confident credulity, when the heart, as yet a novice, freely follows the impulse of youthful sensibility, and bestows itself unreservedly upon the object of disinterested affection! Then, my dear Faublas, then friendship is not a vain name!

The confident of all the secrets of M. de P———, I myself undertook nothing without first intrusting him with my designs; his councils regulated my conduct, mine determined his resolutions; our youth had on pleasures which were not shared, no misfortunes which were not solaced by our mutual attachment.

With what chagrin did I not perceive that fatal

moment arrive, when my friend, obliged by the commands of a father to depart from Warfaw, prepared to take leave of me! We promifed to preferve for ever that lively affection which had conftituted the chief happinefs of our youth, and I rafhly fwore that the paffions of a more advanced age fhould never alter it.

What an immenfe void did the abfence of M. de P——— leave in my heart! At firft it appeared that nothing could compenfate for his lofs; the tendernefs of a father, the careffes of my fifters, affected me but feebly. I thought that no other method remained for me to diffipate the irkfome-nefs of my fituation, than to occupy my leifure moments with fome ufeful purfuit. I therefore cultivated the French language, already efteemed throughout all Europe; I read with delight thofe famous works, the eternal monuments of genius, which it had produced; and I wondered that, notwithftanding fuch an ungrateful idiom, fo many celebrated poets, fo many excellent philofophers and hiftorians, juftly immortalized, had been able to diftinguifh themfelves by its means.

I alfo applied myfelf ferioufly to the ftudy of geometry; I formed my mind in a particular manner to the purfuit of that noble profeffion which makes a hero at the expenfe of one hundred thoufand unfortunates, and which men lefs humane than valiant have called the grand art of war! Several years were employed in thefe purfuits, which are equally difficult and laborious; in fhort, they folely occupied my thoughts. M. de P———, who often wrote to me, no longer received any but fhort replies, and our correfpondence began to languifh by neglect, when at length love finifhed the triumph over friendfhip.

My father had been for a long time intimately connected with count Pulaufki. Celebrated for the aufterity of his manners, famous on account of the inflexibility of his virtues, which were truly republican, Pulaufki, at once a great captain and a brave foldier, had on more than one occafion fignalifed his fiery courage, and his ardent patriotifm.

Inftructed in ancient literature, he had been taught by hiftory the great leffons of a noble difintereffednefs, an immovable conftancy, an abfolute devotion to glory. Like thofe heroes to whom idolatrous, but grateful Rome, elevated altars, Pulaufki would have facrificed all his property to the profperity of his country; he would have fpilled the laft drop of his blood for its defence; he would even have immolated his only, his beloved daughter, Lodoifka.

Lodoifka! **how** beautiful! how lovely! her dear name is always on my lips, her adored remembrance will live for ever in my heart!

My friend, from the firſt moment that I ſaw this fair maid, I lived only for her; I abandoned my ſtudies; friendſhip was entirely forgotten. I conſecrated all my moments to Lodoiſka. My father and her's could not be long ignorant of my attachment; they did not chide me for it;—they muſt have approved it then. This idea appeared to me to be ſo well founded, that I delivered myſelf up, without ſuſpicion, to the ſweet paſſion that enchanted me; and I took my meaſures ſo well that I beheld Lodoiſka almoſt daily, either at home, or in company with my ſiſters, who loved her tenderly:—two ſweet years flew away in this manner.

At length Pulauſki took me one day aſide, and addreſſed me thus: Your father and myſelf have formed great hopes of you, which your conduct has hitherto juſtified; I have long beheld you employing your youth in ſtudies equally uſeful and honourable. To day —— (He here perceived that I was about to interrupt him). What would you ſay? do you think to tell me any thing that I am unacquainted with? do you think that I have occaſion to be the hourly witneſs of your tranſports, to learn how much my Lodoiſka merits to be beloved! It is becauſe I know as well as you the value of my daughter, that you never ſhall obtain her but by meriting her. Young man, learn that it is not sufficient that our foibles should be legitimate to be excusable! those of a good citizen ought to be turned entirely to the profit of his country; love, even love itself, like the basest of the passions, is either despicable or dangerous, if it does not offer to generous hearts an additional motive to excite them towards honour.

Hear me: Our monarch, for a long time in a sickly habit of body, seems at length to approach towards his end. His life, become every day more precarious, has awakened the ambition of our neighbours.* They doubtless prepare to sow divisions among us; and they think, that by overawing our suffrages, they will be enabled to force upon us a king of their own choosing. Foreign troops have already dared to appear on the frontiers of Poland; already two thousand Polish gentlemen have assembled, on purpose to punish their audacious insolence. Go and join yourself with those brave youths; go, and at the end of the campaign, return covered with the blood of our enemies, and shew to Pulaufki a son-in-law worthy of him.

I did not hesitate a single moment; my father approved of my resolutions, but being unable to consent without pain to my precipitate departure,

* The Russians.

he pressed me for a long time against his bosom, while a tender solicitude was depicted in all his looks; his adieus seemed to be inauspicious; the trouble that agitated his heart, seized upon my own; our tears were mingled on his venerable cheeks.

Pulauski, who was present at this moving scene, stoically reproached us for what he termed a weakness. Dry up your tears, said he to me, or preserve them for Lodoiska; it belongs only to childish lovers who separate themselves from each other for five or six months, to weep in this manner! He instructed his daughter, in my presence, both of my departure, and of the motives which had determined me to it. Lodoiska grew pale, sighed, looked at her father with a face suffused with blushes, and then assured me in a trembling voice, that her vows should be offered up for my safe return, and that her happiness depended upon the safety of Lovzinski.

Encouraged in this manner, what dangers had I to fear? I departed accordingly, but in the course of that campaign, there happened nothing worthy of narration; the enemy, equally careful with ourselves to avoid any action which might produce an open war between the two nations, contented themselves with fatiguing us by means of frequent marches: we, on the other hand, bounded our views to following and obferving them; and they only feemed to oppofe themfelves to us, in thofe parts where the open country afforded them an eafy opportunity of making good their retreat.

At the end of the campaign, they prepared to retire, on purpofe to take up their winter quarters in their own country; and our little army, compofed almoft wholly of gentlemen, feparated foon after.

I returned to Warfaw, full of joy and impatience; I thought that Love and Hymen were about to beftow Lodoifka on me.——Alas! I no longer had a father. I learned, on entering the capital, that Lovzinfki died of an apoplexy on the night before my arrival. Thus I was deprived of even the fad confolation of receiving the laft fighs of the moft tender of parents; I could only offer up my forrows at his tomb, which I bathed with my tears!

——It is not, fays Pulaufki to me, who was but little moved with my profound forrow; it is not by means of barren tears that you can do honour to a father fuch as thine. Poland in him regrets a citizen-hero, who would have been of immenfe fervice during the critical moment which now approaches. Worn out with a tedious malady, our monarch has not a fortnight to live, and on the choice of his succeffor depends the happinefs or mifery of our fellow-citizens.

Of all the rights which the death of your father tranfmits to you, the moft noble is undoubtedly that of affifting at the diet, in which you are to reprefent him; it is there where he will revive in you; it is there, where you ought to exhibit a courage infinitely more difficult to be fuftained than that which confifts only in braving death in the field of battle!

The valour of a foldier is nothing more than a common virtue; but they are not ordinary men who on awful emergencies, preferving a tranquil courage, and difplaying an active penetration, difcover the projects of the powerful who cabal, difconcert the enterprifes of the intriguing, and confront the defigns of the factious; who, always firm, incorruptible, and juft, give not their fuffrages but to thofe whom they think moft worthy of them; whom neither gold nor promifes can feduce, whom prayers cannot bend, whom menaces cannot terrify.

Thefe were the virtues which diftinguifhed your father, this is the precious inheritance which you ought to be defirous of fuftaining. The day on which the ftates affemble for the election of a king, will be the epoch on which the pretenfions of many of our fellow-citizens, more occupied with their private interests than jealous of the prosperity of their country, will be manifested, as well as the pernicious designs of the neighbouring powers, whose cruel policy it is to destroy our strength by dividing it.

I am deceived, my friend, if the fatal moment is not fast approaching, which will for ever fix the destiny of our country—its enemies have conspired its ruin; they have secretly prepared for a revolution;——but they shall not confummate their purposes while my arm can sustain a sword! May that God, who is the protector of the republic, prevent all the horrors of a civil war! But that extremity, however frightful it appears, may perhaps become necessary; I flatter myself that it will be but a short, although perhaps a violent crisis, after which the regenerated state will assume its ancient splendor.

You shall second my efforts, Lovzinski; the feeble interests of love ought to disappear before more sacred claims. I cannot present my daughter to you during this awful moment of suspence, when our common country is in danger; but I promise to you, that the first days of peace shall be marked by your union with Lodoiska.

Pulauski did not speak in vain. I felt that I had now more essential duties to fulfil than those of love; but the cares with which my mind was occupied, were hardly able to alleviate my grief. I will even avow to you without blushing, that the sorrow of my sisters, their tender friendship, and the caresses more reserved but no less pleasing of my mistress, made a stronger impression on my heart than the patriotic counsels of Pulauski. I beheld Lodoiska tenderly affected with my irreparable loss, and as much afflicted as myself, at the cruel events which forced us to defer our union; my chagrin, by being thus divided with that lovely woman, seemed insensibly to diminish.

In the mean time the king dies, and the diet is convoked. On the day that it was to open, at the very instant when I was about to repair to the assembly, a stranger presented himself, and desired to speak to me in private. As soon as my attendants were retired, he enters my apartment with precipitation, throws himself into my arms, and tenderly embraces me. It was M. de P———! Ten years, which had elapsed since our separation, had not so much changed his features as to prevent me from recognising him, and testifying my joy and surprise at his unexpected return.

You will be more astonished, says he to me, when you know the cause. I have arrived this instant, and am about to repair to the meeting of the diet;———would it be presuming too much on your friendship to reckon on your vote?

On my vote ! and for whom ?

For myfelf, continues he with vivacity; it is not now time to recount to you the happy revolution that has taken place in my fortune, and which at prefent permits me to entertain fuch exalted hopes: it is fufficient to obferve, that my ambition is at leaft juftified by a majority of fuffrages, and that it is in vain that two feeble rivals would attempt to difpute with me the crown to which I pretend.

Lovzinfki, adds he, embracing me again, if you were not my friend, and if I efteemed you lefs, perhaps I fhould endeavour to dazzle you by means of promifes ; perhaps I fhould recount to you the favours which I intend to heap upon you ; the honourable diftinctions that are referved for you, and the noble and glorious career that is about to offer itfelf to your ambition ;——but I have not any need of feducing, and I only wifh to perfuade you.

I behold it with grief, and you know it as well as myfelf, that for feveral years paft our Poland, become enfeebled, owes its fafety to nothing elfe than the diftruft of the three great powers[*] which furround it, and the defire to enrich themfelves with our fpoils may in one moment reunite our divided enemies !

[*] Ruffia, Pruffia, and the houfe of Auftria.

Let us prevent, if we can, this inauspicious triumvirate from dismembering the republic. Undoubtedly, in more fortunate our ancestors were able to maintain the free of their elections; it is necessary however that we should yield to that necessity which is become inevitable.

Russia will necessarily protect a king, whom she herself has elevated; in receiving the sovereign of her choice, you will defeat the views of that triple alliance which will render our perdition certain, and we shall acquire a powerful ally, who will oppose herself with success to the two enemies that remain to us.

These are reasons which have determined my conduct; I do not abandon part of our rights, but to preserve the most precious of them. I wish not to ascend a fickle throne, but with the intention, by means of a sage policy, to give it stability; I consent not to alter the constitution of the commonwealth, but to preserve the kingdom entire.

We repaired to the diet together; I voted for M. de P———. He in effect obtained the majority of the suffrages; but Pulauski, Zaremba, and some others, declared themselves in favour of prince C———. Nothing was decided amidst the tumult of this first meeting.

When the assembly broke up, M. de P⸺ invited me to accompany him to the palace, which his secret emissaries had already prepared for him in the capital.* We shut ourselves up together during several hours, and renewed the promises of a friendship that should endure for ever. I then too informed M. de P⸺ of my intimate connection with Pulauski, and of my love for Lodoiska. He repaid my confidence with more important communications; he informed me of the events which had led to his approaching grandeur; he explained to me his secret designs; and I left him, convinced that he was less occupied with the desire of his own elevation, than with that of restoring Poland to its ancient prosperity.

Possessed of these ideas, I flew towards my future father-in-law, burning with the desire of adding him to the party of my friend. Pulauski was walking at a great pace up and down the chamber of his daughter, who appeared equally agitated with himself.

Behold, said he to Lodoiska, the moment that he saw me enter, behold that man whom I esteem, and whom you love! He has sacrificed us both to his blind friendship. I was desirous to reply, but

---

* The diet for the election of the kings of Poland was held half a league from Warsaw, in the open air, on the other side of the Vistula, near to the village of Vola.

he went on—You have been connected from your childhood with M. de P——. A powerful faction is about to place him on the throne; you know you are acquainted with his designs; this very morning at the diet, you voted for him—you have deceived me:—but do you think that you shall deceive me with impunity?

I besought him to hear me, and be constrained himself so far as to preserve a stern silence: I then informed him, that M. de P——, whom I had for a long time neglected, had agreeably surprised me by his unexpected return.

Lodoiska appeared charmed to hear me commence my justification.—You shall not deceive me in the same manner as if I were a credulous woman, says Pulauski.—But it signifies not—proceed.

I then recounted to him the particulars of the short conversation that I had with M. de P—— before I repaired to the assembly of the states.

And these are your projects! exclaimed he. M. de P—— sees no other remedy for the misfortunes of his fellow-citizens than their slavery! He proposes this; one of the name of Lovzinski, approves of it; and they despise me so much as to tempt me to enter into this infamous plot! Shall I behold the Russians commanding in our provinces in the name of a Pole?

The Russians, say I with fury; the Russians reign

in my country! On this Pulauſki, advancing towards me with the greateſt impetuoſity, cries out: Perfidious youth! you have deceived me, and you would betray the ſtate! Leave my houſe this very moment, or know that I ſhall order you to be dragged out of it!

I frankly ackowledge to you, Faublas, that an affront ſo cruel, and ſo little merited, diſarmed me of my prudence: in the firſt tranſports of my fury, I placed my hand upon my ſword; and quicker than lightning Pulauſki brandiſhed his in the air.

His daughter, his diſtracted daughter, ruſhed forward, and precipitated herſelf upon me, crying out, Lovzinſki, what are you about to do? On hearing the accents of a voice ſo dear to me, I recalled my wandering reaſon; but I perceived that a ſingle inſtant was about forever to bereave me of my Lodoiſka! She had left me to throw herſelf into the arms of her father. He, cruel man, beheld my grief, and ſtrove to augment it: Go, traitor! ſays he—begone—you behold Lodoiſka for the laſt time!

I returned home in a ſtate of deſperation. The odious names which Pulauſki had laviſhed on me, returned unceaſingly to my reflection. The intereſts of Poland, and thoſe of M. de P——, appeared to be ſo intimately connected together, that I did not perceive in what manner I could betray my fellow-citizens by serving my friend; in the mean time, I was obliged either to abandon him or renounce Lodoiſka forever. What was I to reſolve? what part ſhould I take? I paſſed the whole night in a ſtate of the moſt cruel uncertainty; and when the day appeared, I went towards Pulauſki's houſe, without yet having come to any determination.

The only domeſtic who remained there informed me, that his lord had departed at the beginning of the night, with his daughter, after having firſt diſmiſſed all his people. Think of my deſpair on hearing theſe news. I aſked to what part Pulauſki had retired, but my queſtion was in vain, for he informed me that he was entirely ignorant of the place of his deſtination.

All that I can tell you, ſays he, is, that you had ſcarce gone away yeſterday evening, when we heard a great noiſe in the apartment of his daughter. Still terrified at the ſcene which had taken place between you, I approached the door, and liſtened. Lodoiſka wept: her furious father overwhelmed her with injuries, beſtowed his malediction upon her, and I myſelf heard him exclaim: To love a traitor is to be one! Ungrateful wretch! I ſhall conduct you to a place of ſafety, where you ſhall henceforth be at a diſtance from ſeduction.

Could I any longer doubt the extent of my misery? I instantly called for Boleslas, one of the most faithful of my domestics: I ordered him to place trusty spies about the palace of Pulauski, who should bring an account of every thing that passed there; and commanded that if the count returned to the capital before me, he should follow him wherever he went. Having given these instructions, and not yet despairing of still finding the family at one of their seats in the neighbourhood of the metropolis, I myself set out in pursuit of my mistress.

I accordingly searched through all the domains of Pulauski, and asked concerning Lodoiska, of all the passengers whom I met, but without success. After having spent eight days in fruitless enquiry, I resolved to return to Warsaw, and I was not a little astonished, on my arrival, to find a Russian army encamped on the banks of the Vistula; almost under the very walls of that city.

It was night when I entered the capital: the palaces of the grandees were all illuminated; an immense multitude filled the streets; I heard songs of joy: I beheld wine flowing in rivulets in the public squares; every thing announced to me that Poland had a king.

Boleslas, who expected me with impatience, informed me that Pulauski had returned alone on the fecond day after my departure; and that he had not ftirred from his own palace but to repair to the diet, where in fpite of his efforts, the afcendancy of Ruffia became every day more manifeft. During the laft affembly held this very morning, adds he, M. de P———— united almoft all the fuffrages in his favour, and was about to be declared king, when Pulaufki pronounced the fatal *veto:* at that inftant twenty fabres were brandifhed in the air. The fierce palatine of ————, whom the count had infulted in the former affembly, was the firft to rufh forwards, and gave him a terrible wound on the head. Zaremba, and fome others, flew to the defence of their friend; but all their efforts would have been unable to have faved him, if M. de P————, had not ranged himfelf on their fide, exclaiming at the fame time, that he would facrifice, with his own hand, the firft perfon who dared to approach him. On this the affailants retired. In the mean time Pulaufki, fainting with the lofs of blood, was carried off the field in a ftate of infenfibility. Zaremba departed alfo, fwearing to avenge his friend. Having thus become mafter of the deliberations, the numerous partifans of M. de P———— inftantly proclaimed him fovereign.

Pulaufki, who had been carried to his palace,

was foon reftored to life; and the furgeon who attended him, declared that his wounds, although dangerous, were not mortal. In that ftate, although languifhing under the moft cruel torments, contrary to the advice of all his friends, he ordered himfelf to be lifted into a carriage, and before noon he left Warfaw, accompanied by Mazeppa and a few mal-contents.

It was fcarce poffible to have announced worfe news to me. My friend was upon the throne, but my reconciliation with Pulauski appeared henceforth impoffible, and in all appearance Lodoiska was loft for ever. I knew her father fo well as to be under apprehenfions left he fhould proceed to extremities with his daughter. I was affrighted at the prefent, I durft not look forward towards the future; and my heart was fo devoured with chagrin, that I did not go out, even to felicitate the new king.

One of my people Boleflas difpatched after Pulaufki, returned at the end of the fourth day: he had followed him fifteen leagues from the capital; when about that diftance, Zaremba, who perceived a ftranger at a little diftance from the carriage, began to conceive fufpicions. As they proceeded, four of his followers, who had concealed themfelves behind the ruins of an old houfe, furprifed my courier, and conducted him to Pulaufki.

C

He, with a pistol in his hand, forced him to acknowledge to whom he belonged. I shall send you back to Lovzinski, said the fierce republican, on purpose to announce from me, that he shall not escape my just vengeance. At these words they blind-folded my servant, who could not tell where they had carried him. At the end of four and twenty hours they returned, and tying a handkerchief once more about his eyes, they put him into a carriage, which having stopped at length after a journey of several hours, he was ordered to descend. Scarce had he put his foot upon the ground but his guards departed at a full gallop; on which he removed the bandage, and found himself on the same spot as that on which he had been first arrested.

This intelligence filled me with uneasiness: the menaces of Pulauski terrified me much less on my own account than on Lodoiska's, who remained in his own power: in the midst of his fury he might sacrifice her life! I resolved, therefore, to expose myself to every species of danger, on purpose to discover the retreat of the father, and the prison of his only child.

On the succeeding day, after informing my sisters of my design, I left the capital: Boleslas alone accompanied me, and I passed for his brother. We wandered over all Poland, and I then perceived, that the fears of Pulauſki were but too well juſtified by the event. Under pretence of obliging the inhabitants to take the oath of fidelity to the new king, the Ruſſians, ſcattered about in the provinces, defolated the country, and committed a multitude of exactions in the cities.

After having ſpent three months in vain enquiries, defpairing of being able to find Lodoiska, touched with the moſt lively grief for the fate of my country, and weeping at one and the fame time for her misfortunes and my own, I was about to return to Warſaw, to inform the new king of the exceſſes committed by thofe foreigners in his ſtates, when an adventure that at firſt feemed to be very inaufpicious, forced me to a very different refolution.

The Turks having declared war againſt Ruſſia, the Tartars of Budziac and the Crimea made frequent incurſions into Volhynia, where I then was. Four of thofe robbers attacked us one afternoon, as we were leaving a wood near Oſtropol. I had imprudently neglected to load my piſtols; but I made ufe of my fabre with fo much addreſs and good luck, that in a ſhort time two of them fell covered with wounds. Boleſlas encountered the third; the fourth attacked me with great fury; he gave me a ſlight cut upon the leg, but received a terrible ſtroke in return that difmounted him from his horfe, and felled him to the ground. Boleflas, at the fame moment, perceived himfelf difencumbered from his enemy, who, at the noife made by his comrade's fall, took to flight. He, whom I had juft vanquifhed, then addreffed me in very bad Polifh, and faid : " A brave man like you, ought to be generous. I beg my life of you; inftead of putting me to death, fuccour me, relieve me, bind up my wounds, and affift me to arife."

He demanded quarter with an air fo noble, that I did not hefitate for a moment. I accordingly defcended from my horfe, and Boleflas and myfelf having helped him to arife, we dreffed his wounds. " You behave well," fays the Tartar to me : " you behave well!" As he fpoke, we beheld a cloud of duft, and in a moment after, more than three hundred Tartars rufhed upon us at full fpeed. " Be not afraid, dread nothing," fays he, whom I had fpared; " I am chief of this troop." Accordingly, by means of a fign, he ftops his followers, who were on the point of maffacreing us; and fpeaking to them in their own language, which I was unable to comprehend; they inftantly opened their ranks on purpofe to permit us to pafs.

Brave man, exclaims their captain, addreffing himfelf to me once more, had I not reafon to fay, that you behaved well? You left me my life, and I now fave your's: it is fometimes right to spare an enemy, and even a robber! Hear me, my friend: in attacking you, I followed my profeſſion, and you did your duty in conquering me; let us therefore embrace.—He then adds: the day is waſting, and I would not adviſe you to travel in theſe cantons during the preſent night. My people are about to repair each to his reſpective poſt, and I cannot anſwer for their diſcretion. You perceive a caſtle on a riſing ground, towards the right: it belongs to a certain Pole of the name of Dourlinſki, for whom we have a right eſteem, becauſe he is very rich: Go, demand an aſylum from him; tell him that you have wounded Titſikan, and that Titſikan purſues you. He is acquainted with my name: I have already made him paſs many an uneaſy night. As to the reſt, you may rely on it, that while you remain with him, his caſtle ſhall be ſacred; but be careful not to come forth on any account before the end of three days, and not to remain there longer than eight.—Adieu!

It was with unfeigned pleaſure that we took leave of Titſikan and his companions. The advice of the Tartar was a command; I therefore ſaid to Boleſlas, let us immediately make for the caſtle that he has now pointed out to us; I am well acquainted with this ſame Dourlinſki by name. Pulauſki has ſometimes ſpoken to me concerning him; he perhaps is not ignorant of the place to which the count has retired, and it is not impossible but that with a little addrefs we may be able to draw the fecret from him. I fhall fay at all events that we are fent by Pulauski, and this recommendation will be of more fervice to us than that of Titfikan: in the mean time, Boleflas, do not forget that I am your brother, and be fure not to difcover me.

We foon arrived at the ditch of the caftle; the fervants of Dourlinski demanded who we were: I anfwered that we were come from Pulauski, and wifhed to fpeak to their lord, and that we had been attacked by robbers, who were ftill in purfuit of us. The drawbridge was accordingly let down; and having entered, we were informed that at prefent we could not fee Dourlinski, but that on the next day at ten o'clock he fhould give us audience. They then demanded our arms, which we delivered up without any difficulty, and Boleflas foon after took an opportunity of looking at my wound, which was found to be but fuperficial.

In a fhort time a frugal repaft was ferved up for us, in the kitchen. We were afterwards conducted to a lower chamber, where two bad beds were prepared for us. The domeftics then left us without any light, and immediately locked the door of the apartment.

I could not clofe my eyes during the whole night. Titfikan had given me but a flight wound, but that which my heart had received was fo very deep! At day break, I became impatient in my prifon, and wifhed to open the fhutters, but they were nailed up. I attacked them, however, fo vigoroufly, that the faftening gave way ; and I beheld a very fine park. The window being low, I cleared it at a leap, and in a fingle inftant found myfelf in the gardens of the Polifh chieftain.

After having walked about for a few minutes, I fat down on a ftone bench, which was placed at the foot of a tower, whofe ancient architecture I had been fome time confidering. I remained for a few feconds enveloped in reflection, when a tile fell at my feet. I thought it had dropped from the roof of this old building ; and, to avoid the effects of a fimilar accident, I went and placed myfelf at the other end of the feat. A few moments after, a fecond tile fell by my fide. The circumftance appeared furprifing: I arofe with fome degree of inquietude, and attentively examined the tower. I perceived at about twenty-five or thirty feet from the ground, a narrow opening. On this I picked up the tiles which had been thrown at me, and on the firft I difcovered the following words, written with a bit of plaifter.

Lovzinfki, is it you ! Do you ftill live !

And on the second these:
Deliver me! save Lodoiska.

It is not possible for you, my dear Faublas, to conceive how many different sentiments occupied my mind at one and the same time: my astonishment, my joy, my grief, my embarrassment, cannot be expressed. I examined once more the prison of Lodoiska, and plotted in my own mind how I could procure her liberty. She at length threw down another tile, and I read as follows:

"At midnight, bring me paper, ink, and pens; and to-morrow, an hour after sun-rise, come and receive a letter.——Begone."—

Having returned towards my chamber, I called Boleslas, who assisted me in re-entering through the window. I then informed my faithful servant, of the unexpected accident that had put an end to my wanderings, and redoubled my inquietude.

How could I penetrate into this tower? How could we procure arms? By what means were we to deliver Lodoiska from captivity? How could we carry her off under the eye of Dourlinski, in the midst of his people, and from a fortified castle! and supposing that so many obstacles were not unsurmountable, could I attempt such a difficult enterprize during the short delay prescribed by Titsikan?

Did not the Tartar enjoin me to stay with Dourlinski three days, but not to remain longer than eight?

Would it not be to expose ourselves to the attacks of the enemy, to leave this castle before the third, or after the expiration of the eighth day? Should I release my dear Lodoiska from a prison, on purpose to deliver her into the hands of robbers, to be forever separated from her by slavery or by death? This would be a horrible idea!

But wherefore was she confined in such a frightful prison? The letter which she had promised would doubtless instruct me: it was therefore necessary to procure paper, pen and ink. I accordingly charged Boleslas with this employment, and began to prepare myself for acting the delicate part of an emissary of Pulauski in the presence of Dourlinski.

It was broad daylight when they came to set us at liberty, and inform us, that Dourlinski was at leisure, and wished to see us.—We accordingly presented ourselves before him with great confidence; and we were introduced to a man of about sixty years of age, whose reception was blunt, and whose manners were repulsive. He demanded who we were. My brother and myself, replied I, belong to count Pulauski. My master has entrusted me with a secret commission to you. My brother accompanies me on another account. Before I explain, I muſt be in private, for I am charged not to ſpeak but to you alone.

It is very well, replies Dourlinſki : your brother may retire, and you alſo, addreſſing himſelf to his ſervants, begone! As to him here (pointing to a perſon who was his confident) he muſt remain, and you may ſpeak any thing before him.

Palauſki has ſent me——I ſee very well that he has ſent you, ſays the palatine, interrupting me——to demand of you——What ?——news of his daughter.—News of his daughter! Did Pulauſki ſay ſo ?——Yes, my lord ſaid that his daughter was here.—I perceived that Dourlinſki inſtantly grew pale; he then looked towards his confident, and ſurveyed me for ſome time in ſilence.

You aſtoniſh me, rejoins he at length.—In confiding a ſecret of this importance to you, it neceſſarily follows that your maſter muſt have been very imprudent.

No more than you, my lord, for have not you alſo a confident ? Grandees would be much 'to be pitied if they could not rely upon any of their domeſtics. Pulauſki has charged me to inform you, that Lovzinſki has already ſearched through a great part of Poland, and that he will undoubtedly viſit theſe cantons.

If he dares to come here, replies he with great vivacity, I will provide a lodging for him, which he shall inhabit for some time.—Do you know this Lovzinski?

I have often seen him at my master's house in Warsaw.—They say he is handsome.

He is well made, and about my height.

His person?—is prepossessing; it is——

He is a wretch, adds he, interrupting me in a great passion——O that he were but to fall into my hands!

My lord, they say that he is brave—

He! I will wager any sum of money that he is only calculated to seduce women!—O that he would but fall into my hands! Then assuming a less ferocious tone, he continued thus: It is a long time since Pulauski wrote to me—where is he at present?

My lord, I have precise orders not to answer that question: all that I dare to say is, that he has the strongest reasons for neither discovering the place of his retreat, nor writing to any person, and that he will soon come and explain them to you in person.

Dourlinski appeared exceedingly astonished at this information: I even thought that I could discover some symptoms of fear in his countenance. At length, looking at his confident, who seemed equally embarrassed with himself, he proceeded. You say that Pulauski will come here soon? Yes, my lord, in about a fortnight, or a little later. On this he again turned to his attendant; but in a short time affecting as much calmness as he had before discovered embarrassment:—Return to your master, added he; I am sorry to have nothing but bad news to communicate to him—tell him that Lodoiska is no longer here. I myself became surprised in my turn at this information. What! my lord, Lodoiska——

Is not longer here, I tell you!—to oblige Pulauski, whom I esteem, I undertook, although with great repugnance, the task of confining his daughter in my castle: nobody but myself and he (pointing to his confident) knew that she was here. It is about a month since we went, as usual, to carry her provisions for the day, but there was nobody to be found in the apartment. I am ignorant how it happened; but what I know well is, that she has escaped, for I have heard nothing of her since.—She must undoubtedly have gone to join Lovzinski at Warsaw, if perchance the Tartars have not intercepted her in her journey.

My astonishment on this became extreme. How could I reconcile that which I had seen in the garden, with that which Dourlinski now told me? There was some mystery in this business, which I became exceedingly impatient to be acquainted with; I was however extremely careful not to exhibit any appearance of doubt. My lord, said I, this is bad news for my master!—Undoubtedly, but it is not my fault.

My lord, I have a favour to ask of you.

Let me hear it.——The Tartars are ravaging the neighbourhood of your castle—they attacked us——we escaped, as it were, by a miracle. Will you permit my brother and myself to remain here only for the space of two days?

For two days only I give my consent.

Where do they lodge? says he to his attendant.

In an apartment below ground, was the reply.

Which overlooks my gardens? rejoins Dourlinski, interrupting him with great agitation.

The shutters are well fastened, adds the other.

No matter——You must put them elsewhere. These words made me tremble.

It is not possible, but——continues the confident, and then whispered the rest of the sentence in his ear.

Right, says the baron; and let it be done instantly. Then, addressing himself to me, he says, your brother and you must depart the day after to-morrow; before you go you shall see me again, and I will give you a letter for Pulauski.

I then went to rejoin Belesias in the kitchen,

where he was at breakfaft, who foon after prefented me with a little bottle full of ink, feveral pens, and fome fheets of paper, which he had procured without difficulty. I panted with defire to write to Lodoiska; and the only difficulty that now remained, was to find a commodious place, where I might not be difcovered by the curiofity of Dourlinski's people.

They had already informed Boleflas that we could not again be admitted into the apartment where we had fpent the preceding night, until the time fhould arrive when we were to retire to reft. I foon, however, bethought myfelf of a ftratagem which fucceeded to admiration.

The fervants were drinking with my pretended brother, and politely invited me to help them to empty a few flasks.

I fwallowed, with a good grace, feveral glaffes of bad wine in fucceffion: in a few minutes my legs feemed to totter under me; my tongue faultered: I related a hundred pleafant and improbable tales to the joyous company; in a word, I acted the *drunken man* fo well, that Boleflas himfelf became a dupe to my fcheme, aud actually trembled left, in a moment when I feemed difpofed to communicate every thing, my secret fhould efcape.

Gentlemen, faid he, to the aftonifhed bacchanals, my brother's head is not very ftrong to-day; it is perhaps in confequence of his wound; let us not therefore, either fpeak to or drink any more with him; for I am afraid of his health, and indeed you would oblige me exceedingly if you would affift me to carry him to his bed.—To his own bed? fays one of them, that is impoffible! But I will moft willingly lend him my chamber. They accordingly laid hold of me, and conveyed me into a garret, of which a bed, a table, and a chair formed the fole movables. Having fhut me up in this paltry apartment, they inftantly left me. This was all that I wanted, for the moment that I was alone, I immediately fat down to write a long letter to Lodoiska.

I began, by fully juftifying myfelf from the crimes of which I had been accufed by Pulauski: I then recounted every thing that had occured fince the firft moment of our feparation, until that when I had entered the caftle of Dourlinski: I detailed the particulars of my converfation with the baron: I concluded, by affuring her of the moft tender and the moft refpectful paffion, and fwore to her, that the moment fhe gave me the neceffary information concerning her fituation, I would expofe myfelf to every danger in order to finifh her horrid captivity.

As foon as my letter was fealed, I delivered myfelf up to a variety of reflections, which threw me into a ftrange perplexity. Was it actually Lodoiska who had thrown thofe tiles into the garden? Would Pulauski have had the injuftice to punifh his daughter for an attachment which he himfelf had approved? Would he have had the inhumanity to plunge her into a frightful prifon? And even if the hatred he had fworn to me, had blinded him fo much, how was it poffible, that Dourlinski would thus have condefcended to have become the minifter of his vengeance?

But, on the other hand, for thefe three laft long months, on purpofe to difguife myfelf, I had only worn tattered clothes: the fatigues of a tedious journey, and my chagrin, had altered me greatly; and who but a miftrefs could have been able to difcover Lovzinski in the gardens of Dourlinski? Befides, had I not feen the name of Lodoiska traced upon the tile? Had not Dourlinski himfelf acknowledged that Lodoiska had been a prifoner with him? Is it true, he had added that fhe had made her efcape; but was not this incredible? And wherefore that hatred which Dourlinski had avowed againft me, without knowing my perfon? What occafioned that look of inquietude, when it was told him, that the emiffaries of Pulauski occupied a chamber that looked into his garden? And why, above all, that appearance of terror, when I announced to him the approaching arrival of my pretended mafter?

All these circumstances were well calculated to throw me into the greatest agitation. I ruminated over this frightful and mysterious adventure, which it was impossible for me to explain. For two hours, I unceasingly put new questions to myself, to which I was exceedingly embarrassed to make any reply; when at length Boleslas came to see if I had recovered from my debauch. I had but little difficulty in convincing him that my inebriety was mere affectation; after which we went down together to the kitchen, where we spent the rest of the day. What a night!—My dear Faublas, no one in my whole life ever appeared so long, not even that which followed.

At length the attendants conducted us to our chamber, where they shut us up, as on the former occasion, without any light: it was yet two tedious hours until midnight. At the first stroke of the clock, we gently opened the shutters and the casement. I then prepared to jump into the garden; but my embarrassment was equal to my despair, when I found myself obstructed by means of iron bars. "Behold," said I to Boleslas, "what the cursed confident of Dourlinski whispered in his ear! behold what his odious master approved, when he said, *let it be done instantly!* behold what they have been working at during the day! it was on this account that they prevented us from entering the chamber."

" My lord, they have ftood on the outfide," replied Boleflas ; " for they have not perceived that the fhutter has been forced."

" Alas! whether they have perceived it or not," exclaimed I, with violence, " what does it fignify? This fatal grating deftroys all my hopes; it infures the flavery of Lodoiska—it infures my death."

" Yes, without doubt, it infures thy death!" repeats a perfon at the fame time opening the door; and immediately after, Dourlinski, preceded by feveral armed men, and followed by others carrying flambeaux, enters our prifon *fabre in hand*. " Traitor!" exclaims he, while addreffing himfelf to me with a look in which fury was vifibly depicted, " I have heard all—I know who you are, —your fervant has difcovered your name. Tremble! Of all the enemies of Lovzinski, I am the moft implacable!"

" Search them," continued he, turning to his attendants: they accordingly rufhed in upon me; and as I was without arms, I made an ufelefs refiftance. They accordingly robbed me of my papers, and of the letter which I had juft written to Lodoiska. Dourlinski exhibited a thoufand figns of impatience while reading it, and was fcarce able to contain himfelf.

"Lovzinski," fays he to me, endeavouring to fmother his rage, " I already deferve all your hatred; I fhall foon merit it ftill more: in the mean time, you muft remain with your worthy confident in this chamber, to which you are fo partial."

After uttering thefe words, he left me; and having double locked the door, he placed a centinel on the outfide, and another in the garden, oppofite to the window.

Figure to yourfelf the horrible fituation into which Boleflas and myfelf were now plunged. My misfortunes were at their height; but thofe of Lodoiska affected me infinitely more than my own! How great muft be her uneafinefs! She expects Lovzinski, and Lovzinski abandons her! But no—Lodoiska knows me too well; fhe can never fufpect me of fuch bafe perfidy. Lodoiska! fhe will judge of her lover by herfelf; fhe will think that Lovzinski partakes her lot, fince he does not fuccour her—Alas! the very certainty of my misfortunes will augment her own.

On the next day, they gave us provifions through the grating of our window; and by the quality of the viands which they furnifhed us with, Boleflas augured the moft finifter events. Being however lefs unhappy than myfelf, he fupported his fate much more courageously. He offered me my share of the mean repast which he was about to make; I could not eat: he pressed me; but it was in vain! for existence was become an unsupportable burden to me.

"Ah! live! said he at length, shedding a torrent of tears: "live; and if not for Boleslas, let it be for Lodoiska!" These words made the most lively impression upon my mind; they even re-animated my courage: and hope having once more re-entered my heart, I embraced my faithful servant. "O my friend!" exclaimed I at the same time with transport, " my true friend! I have been the occasion of thy ruin, and yet my misfortunes affect thee more than thine own! Yes, Boleslas! yes! I will live for Lodoiska; I will live for thee: if just heaven shall restore me to my fortune and rank, you shall see that your master is not ungrateful!" We now embraced once more.

Ah! my dear Faublas, how much do misfortunes connect men together! how sweet it is, when one suffers, to hear another unfortunate address a word of consolation to him!

We had groaned in this prison for no less than twelve days, when several ruffians came to drag me forth on purpose to conduct me to Dourlinski. Boleslas wished to follow, but they repulsed him with violence: however they permitted me to speak to him for a single moment. I then drew from a private pocket a ring which I had worn for ten years, and said to Boleslas:—" This ring was given me by M. de P. when we were at college together at Warsaw: take it, my friend, and preserve it for my sake. If Dourlinski this day consummates his treason by my assassination, and, if he should at length permit you to leave this castle, go, find your king, recal to his memory our ancient attachment, recount my misfortunes to him; he will recompence you, and succour Lodoiska. Adieu, my friend!"

After this, I was conducted to the apartment of Dourlinski. As soon as the door opened, I perceived a lady in a chair, who had just fainted away. I approached her—it was Lodoiska! Heavens! how much did I find her altered!— but she was still handsome! "Barbarian!" exclaimed I, addressing myself to Dourlinski; and at the voice of her lover, Lodoiska recovered her senses.

"Ah, my dear Lovzinski," says she, looking wistfully at me, " do you know what this infamous wretch has proposed? do you know at what price he has offered me your liberty?"

" Yes," cries the furious chieftain, " yes, I am determined upon it: you see that he is in my power; and if in three days I do not obtain my wishes, he shall be no more!" I endeavoured to throw myself on my knees at the feet of Lodoiska; but my guards prevented me: " I behold you again, and all my ills are forgotten, Lodoiska—death has now no longer any thing terrifying in its aspect!"

" Wretch," added I, looking sternly at Dourlinski, " know that Pulauski will avenge his daughter! know that the king will avenge his friend!"

" Let him be carried away," was the only reply made by the ferocious palatine.

" Ah!" exclaims Lodoiska, " my love has been your ruin!" I was about to answer, but the attendants dragged me out, and re-conducted me to prison.

Boleslas received me with inexpressible transports of joy; he avowed to me that he thought me lost forever, and I recounted to him how my death was but deferred. The scene of which I had just been a witness, confirmed all my suspicions; it was evident that Pulauski was ignorant of the unworthy treatment which his daughter experienced; it was also evident that Dourlinski, old, amorous, and jealous, was determined, at any rate, to satisfy his passions.

In the mean time, two of the days allowed

by Dourlinſki for the determination of Lodoiska, had already expired; we were now in the midſt of the night which preceded the fatal third one; I could not ſleep, and I was walking haſtily about my priſon. All at once I heard the cry of To arms! to arms!" The moſt frightful howlings prevailed on the outſide, and a great commotion took place within the caſtle. Boleſlas and I were able to diſtinguiſh the voice of Dourlinski, calling and encouraging his followers; and we ſoon diſtinctly heard the claſhing of the ſwords; the cries of the wounded, and the groans of the dying. The noiſe which at firſt was very great, ſeemed at length to die away. It recommenced ſoon after; it redoubled; and at length we heard the ſhout of "Victory!"

To this frightful tumult, a ſtill more frightful ſilence enſues. In a ſhort time a low crackling ſound is heard to approach us; the air ſeems to hiſs with violence; the night becomes leſs dark; the trees in the garden aſſume a red and warm tint; we fly to the window; the flames are devouring the caſtle of Dourlinski! They approach the chamber in which we were confined, from all ſides; and to overwhelm me with new horror, the moſt piercing ſhrieks are uttered from the tower in which I knew that Lodoiska was impriſoned!

The fire becoming every moment more violent,

was about to communicate to the chamber in which we were shut up, and the flames already began to curl around the base of the tower in which Lodoiska was immured!

Lodoiska uttered the most dreadful groans, to which I answered by cries of fury. Boleslas rushed from one part of the prison to another like a madman; he sent forth the most terrible howlings; he attempted to burst open the door with his hands and feet. As for myself, I remained at the window, and shook, amidst my transports of fury, those massive iron bars which I was unable to bend.

All of a sudden, the domestics, who had lately mounted the battlements, descend with precipitation, and open the gates: we heard the voice of Dourlinski himself begging for quarter. The victors instantly precipitate themselves amidst the flames; and being at length attracted by our cries, they force open the door of our prison with their hatchets.

By their dress and their arms, I knew them to be Tartars: their chief arrives—it is Titsikan!

Ah! ah! exclaims he; it is my brave friend!

I instantly threw myself on his neck :—Titsikan! Lodoiska!——a lady!——the fairest of women!——in that tower!—about to be burnt alive!

These were the incoherent expressions by which I made my feelings known.

The Tartar inftantly gives the word of command to his foldiers: they fly to the tower: I fly along with them: Boleflas follows us. They burft open the doors; and near to an old pillar we difcover a narrow, winding ftaircafe, filled with fmoke.

The Tartars, affrighted at the danger, ftart back: I prepare to afcend.

Alas! what are you about? exclaims Boleflas. To live or die with Lodoiska!

And I will either live or die with my mafter! was the reply of my generous fervant.

I rufh on—he follows me! At the risk of fuffocation we afcend about forty fteps: by the light of the flames we difcover Lodoiska in a corner of her prifon; who feebly utters: Who is it that approaches me?

It is Lovzinski! it is your lover!

Joy inftantly lends her new ftrength; fhe rifes and flies into my arms: we carry her away; we defcend a few fteps; but volumes of fmoke now fill the ftaircafe, and we are forced to re-afcend with precipitation. At that very inftant too, a part of the tower gives way!—Boleflas utters a dreadful fhriek, and Lodoiska falls into a fwoon.

Faublas, that which was on the point of deftroying, faved us! The flames, formerly fmothered, began to extend with greater rapidity;

but the smoke was dissipated.—Laden with our precious burden, Boleslas and I descend in haste.—My friend, I do not exaggerate; every step trembled under our feet! the walls were all on fire! At length we arrived at the gate of the tower; Titsikan, trembling for our safety, was expecting us there: Brave men! exclaimed he, on seeing us appear again.——I place Lodoiska at his feet, and fall down lifeless by her side!

I remained nearly an hour in this situation. They tremble for my life; and Boleslas weeps aloud. I again recover my senses, on hearing the voice of Lodoiska, who, returning to herself, calls me her deliverer. The appearance of every thing was altered; the tower was entirely in ruins. The Tartars, however, had stopped the progress of the flames; they had destroyed one part of the castle, on purpose to save the remainder; in fine, we had been carried into a large saloon, where we were surrounded by Titsikan and some of his soldiers. Others of them were occupied in pillaging and in bringing away the gold, silver, jewels, plate, and all the precious effects which the flames had spared.

Near to us, Dourlinski, loaded with fetters, and uttering repeated groans, beheld this heap of riches, of which he was about to be despoiled. Rage, terror, despair, all the passions which can tear the heart of a villain fuffering under punifh-ment, were vifibly depicted in his wild and wandering looks. He ftruck the earth with fury, dafhed his clenched hands againft his forehead, and, uttering the moft horrible blafphemies, he reproached heaven for its juft vengeance.

In the mean time, my lovely miftrefs holds my hand clafped in her's. Alas, fays fhe, at length, with tears in her eyes, alas! you have faved my life, and your own is ftill in danger! Nay, even if we efcape death, flavery awaits us!

No, no, Lodoiski, be comforted, Titfikan is no my enemy; Titfikan will put a period to our misfortunes—

Undoubtedly, if I am able, exclaims the Tartar, interrupting me: you are in the right, brave man! (adds he) I fee that you are not dead, and I am happy: you always fay and do good things; and you have there (turning to Boleflas), you have there a friend who feconds you admirably.

On this I embrace Boleflas:—yes, Titfikan, yes, I have a friend, who fhall always be dear to me!—

The Tartar again interrupts me: What! were not you both confined in an apartment below ground, and was not this lady in a tower? What was the reafon of this? I will lay any wager, continues he with a fmile, that you have taken

E 2

this female from that old lecher (pointing to Dourlinski) and you are in the right; for he is a dotard, and she is beautiful! Come—inform me of every thing.

I now difcover my name to Titfikan, that of Lodoiska's father, and every particular that occurred to me until that moment. It belongs to Lodoiska, I obferve in conclufion, to make us acquainted with what fhe has been obliged to fuffer from the infamous Dourlinski, ever fince fhe has been in his caftle!

You know, replies Lodoiska, that my father obliged me to leave Warfaw, on the day that the diet was opened. He firft conducted me to the territories of the palatine of ———, at only twenty leagues diftance from the capital, to which he returned, on purpofe to affift at the meeting of the ftates.

On that very day, when M. de P—— was proclaimed king, Pulauski took me from the caftle of the palatine, and conducted me here, thinking that I fhould be better concealed. He charged Dourlinski to guard me with extraordinary ftrictnefs; and, above all things, to take efpecial care to prevent Lovzinski from difcovering the place of my retreat. He then left me, as he informed me, on purpofe to affemble and to encourage the good citizens to defend his country, and to punish traitors. Alas! these important avocations have made him forget his daughter, for I have never seen him since.

A few days after his departure, I began to perceive, that the visits of Dourlinski had been more frequent than usual; in a short time, he hardly ever quitted the apartment which had been assigned me for a prison. He deprived me, under some trifling pretexts, of the only female attendant, whom my father had left me; and to prevent any person (as he said) from knowing that I was in his castle, he himself brought me the food necessary for my subsistence, and passed whole days along with me.

You cannot conceive, my dear Lovzinski, how much I suffered from the continual presence of a man who was odious to me, and whose infamous designs I was suspicious of; he even dared to explain himself to me one day; but I assured him, that my hate should always be the price of his tenderness, and that his unworthy conduct had drawn upon him my sovereign contempt.

He answered me coldly, that in time I would accustom myself to see him, and to suffer his assiduities; nay, he did not in the least alter his usual conduct, for he entered my chamber in the morning, and never retired until night. Separated from all I loved, I had not even the feeble consolation of being able to enjoy the sweet recollection of past happiness. A witness to my misfortunes, Dourlinski took pleasure in augmenting them.

Pulauski, says he to me, commands a body of Polish troops; Lovzinski betraying his country, which he does not love, and a woman concerning whom he is indifferent, serves in the Russian army, where he will be cut off during some bloody engagement: besides, if he survives, it is evident that nothing can ever reconcile your father to him.

A few days after, he came on purpose to announce to me, that Pulauski, during the night, had attacked the Russians in their camp; and that, amidst the confusion that ensued, my lover had fallen by the hand of my father. The cruel palatine even made me read a narrative of this event, drawn up with every appearance of truth, in a kind of public gazette, which doubtless he had procured to be printed expressly for the purpose: besides, on perceiving the barbarous joy which he affected on this occasion, I thought the news but too true.

Pitiless tyrant, cried I, you enjoy my tears and my despair; but cease to persecute me, or you will soon see that the daughter of Pulauski is herself able to avenge her own injuries.

One evening that he had left me sooner than usual, after I retired to bed, I heard my door open very softly. By the light of a lamp which I kept always burning, I beheld my tyrant advancing towards my bed. As there was no crime of which I did not believe him to be capable, I had foreseen this event; and I had even taken measures to render it unsuccessful. I accordingly armed myself with a long, sharp knife, which I had the precaution to conceal beneath my pillow; I overwhelmed the wretch with the reproaches which he so justly merited; and I vowed, if he dared to advance, that I would poignard him with my own hand.

He retired, with surprise and affright visibly delineated on his countenance; I am tired, said he, as he went out, with experiencing nothing but scorn; and if I were not afraid of being overheard, you should soon perceive what a woman's arm could effect against mine! But I know a way of vanquishing your pride! By and by you will think yourself but too happy in being able to purchase your pardon, by the most humiliating submissions.

He now withdrew. A few moments after, his confident entered with a pistol in his hand. I must, however, do him the justice to say, that he wept while he announced to me the orders of his lord.

Dress yourself, madam; you must instantly

follow me!—This was all that he was able to say to me.

He then conducted me to that very tower, where, without you, I should this morning have perished: he shut me up in that horrible prison: it was there that I had languished for more than a month, without fire, without the light of heaven, and almost without clothes; with bread and water for my food; for my bed a few trusses of straw: this was the deplorable state to which the only daughter of a grandee of Poland was reduced!

You shudder, brave stranger, and yet believe me, when I assure you, that I do not recount to you any more than a small part of my sufferings. One thing, however, rendered my misery less insupportable: I no longer beheld my tyrant. While he expected with tranquility that I should solicit my pardon, I passed whole days and nights calling on the name of my father, and in bewailing my lover! * * * * *
* * * * O Lovzinski!! with what astonishment was I seized; with what joy was my soul penetrated, on that day when I once more beheld you in the gardens of Dourlinski!! * * * * *
* * * * * * *

Titsikan was listening to the story of our misfortunes, with which he appeared to be deeply affected, when one of his centinels approached, and founded an alarm. He immediately left us in great hafte, on purpofe to run to the draw-bridge. We heard a great tumult, and began already to prefage fome inaufpicious event.

While we remained plunged in confternation, —Lovzinski, Lodoiska, cowardly and perfidious pair! exclaims Dourlinski, unable to contain his joy—you have hoped to be able to elude my vengeance, and efcape my chaftifement. Tremble, you are once more about to fall into my hands. At the noife of my captivity and misfortunes, the neighbouring nobility are undoubtedly affembled, and have now come to fuccour me.

—They can only revenge you, villain!—cries Boleflas, interrupting him in the midft of his threats, and feizing at the fame time, an iron bar, with which he prepared to knock him down; I, however, inftantly interpofed, and prevented him from executing this act of juftice.

Titfikan returned in a few minutes: it is only a falfe alarm, faid he to us: it is nothing more than a fmall detachment which I difpatched yefterday, on purpofe to fcour the country—they had orders to rejoin me here; and they have brought me fome prifoners: every thing is quiet, and the neighbourhood does not appear to be in the leaft commotion.

While Titſikan yet ſpoke to me, a number of unfortunates, whoſe luckleſs fate had delivered them into the hands of the enemy, were dragged before him. We firſt beheld five, who being unbound, walked by the ſide of their conquerors, with a downcaſt and malancholy aſpect. The Tartars told us, that one of their companions had been overcome with great difficulty, and that was the reaſon why he was bound hand and foot!

The ſixth now appeared: O heavens! it is my father! exclaims Lodoiſka, running at the ſame time towards him. I, too, throw myſelf at the feet of Pulauſki.

Are you Pulauſki? ſays the Tartar chieftain, 'tis well—the event is lucky! Believe me, my friend, it is not more than a quarter of an hour ſince I firſt heard of you. I know however that you are proud and hot-headed, but no matter; I eſteem you: you poſſeſs both courage and abilities; your daughter is beautiful, and does not want for underſtanding; Lovzinski is brave—braver than myſelf, as I have already experienced. Attend to what I am about to ſay——

Pulauski, motionleſs with aſtoniſhment, ſcarcely heard the ſound of the Tartar's voice; and ſtruck, at the ſame time, with the ſtrange ſpectacle that offered itſelf to his view, he began to conceive the moſt horrible ſuſpicions.

He repulsed my caresses with the most significant disgust: Wretch! exclaims he at length, you have betrayed your country, a woman who loved you, a man who prided himself in calling you his son-in-law; it was only wanting to fill up the measure of your crimes, that you should league with robbers.

With robbers! cries Titsikan—with robbers indeed, if it so please you to call us; but you yourself must acknowledge that description of people to be good for something; for without me, perhaps, your daughter by to-morrow's sun, would no longer have been a maiden. Be not alarmed, says he, addressing himself to me: but I know that he is proud, and I therefore am not angry.

We had, by this time, placed Pulauski in a chair; his daughter and myself bathed his manacles with our tears: but he still continued to frown at, and to overwhelm me with reproaches.

What, in the name of the devil, would you wish for? cries the Tartar, once more addressing his captive: I tell you that Lovzinski is a brave man, whom I intend to see married; and as for your Dourlinski, he is a rogue, whom I am about to order to be hanged.

I repeat to you, once more, that you alone are

more *hot-headed* than us three put together. But, hear me, and let us finish this business; for it is necessary that I should depart. You belong to me, by the most incontestible right, that of the sword. But if you promise me, upon your honour, that you will be sincerely reconciled to Lovzinski, and give your daughter to him for a wife, I will restore you to your liberty.

He who can brave death, replies the haughty Pulauski, can support slavery. My daughter shall never be the wife of a traitor.

Do you love better, that she should be a Tartar's mistress?—If you do not promise to give her, within the space of eight days, to this brave man, I myself shall espouse her this very night! When I am weary of you and of her, I will sell you to the Turks. Your daughter is handsome enough to find admittance into the *haram* of a bashaw: and you yourself may, perhaps, superintend the kitchen of some janissary.

My life is in your hands; do with it whatsoever you please. If Pulauski falls beneath the sword of a Tartar, he will be lamented, and even his enemies will agree, that he merits a more glorious destiny: but if he were to consent——No! no! I rather choose—I prefer death!

I do not desire your death! I wish only that Lovzinski should espouse Lodoiska. What!—shall my prisoner give the law to me? By my sabre!—this dog of a Christian—but I am in the wrong—he is furious, and is assuredly deprived of his reason.

I now beheld the Tartar's eyes sparkle with fury, and therefore recalled to his memory the promise he had made me, that he would not give way to his passion.

Undoubtedly! but this man wearies out the patience of a favourite of our prophet! I am but a robber!—Yet, Pulauski, I repeat it to you again, that it is my command that Lovzinski espouse your daughter. By my sabre, he has fairly gained her; but for him she had been burnt last night.

But for him!

Yes, behold those ruins; there stood a tower in that place; it was on fire, and no person dared to ascend it: he, however, mounted the staircase, attended by Boleslas—and they saved your daughter?

Was my daughter in that tower?

Yes, that hoary villain had confined her there—that hoary villain, who attempted to violate her!—Some of you must relate the whole to him; but make haste, as it is necessary that he should decide it instantly: I have business elsewhere, for I do not intend that your militia* shall furprife me here: it is otherwife in the plains; there I fhould laugh at them.

While Titfikan ordered the rich booty which he had taken, to be ftowed in little covered waggons, Lodoifka informed her father of the crimes of Dourlinfki, and mingled the recital of our affection fo artfully with the hiftory of our misfortunes, that nature and gratitude at one and the fame time befieged the heart of Pulaufki.

Affected in the moft lively manner with the misfortunes of his daughter, and fenfible of the important fervices which I had rendered her: he embraces Lodoifka, and at length beholding me without refentment, he feemed to wait impatiently for an opportunity to be reconciled to me.

O Pulaufki! I exclaim, you whom heaven hath left me on purpofe to confole me for the lofs of the beft of fathers: you for whom I have an equal friendfhip and veneration: why haft thou condemned thy children unheard. Why haft thou fuppofed a man who adores thy daughter, guilty of the moft horrible treafon?

When my vows were offered up in favour of that prince who now fills the throne, I fwear to

---

* The troops ftationed on purpofe to watch over the fafety of the frontiers of Podolia and Volhinia, and preferve them from the incurfions of the Tartars, are called *Quartuaires*.

you, Pulaufki, by her whom I love fo tenderly, that I looked upon his elevation to be an event highly aufpicious to the happinefs, the fafety, and the profperity of my country.

The misfortunes which my youth did not forefee, thy experience had anticipated: but becaufe I have been wanting in prudence, ought you to accufe me of perfidy? Ought you to have reproached me for loving my friend? Can you now look upon it as a crime, that I ftill give him my efteem? For the three laft months, I have beheld the misfortunes of my country in the fame point of view as yourfelf; like you, I have mourned over them; but I am fure that the king is ftill ignorant of their extent, and I fhall go to Warfaw on purpofe to inform him of all that I have feen.

Pulaufki here interrupts me:—It is not there that you ought to repair: you tell me that M. de P—— is not informed of the wrongs done to his native country, and I believe you; but whether he is acquainted with, or whether he is entirely ignorant of them, is now but of little confequence. Infolent foreigners, cantoned throughout our provinces, ftrive to maintain themfelves in the republic, even againft the king, whom they have caufed to be elected. It is no longer in the power of an impotent or a mal-content king, to chafe the Ruffians from my country!

Let us truft only to ourfelves, Lovzinfki; and let us either avenge our country, or die in her defence. I have affembled 4000 noble Poles in the palatine of Lublin, who wait but for the return of their general to march againft the Ruffians; follow me to my camp——on this condition I am your friend, and my daughter fhall be your wife.

Pulaufki, I am ready to obey you: I fwear to follow your fortunes, and to participate in your dangers. And think not that it is Lodoifka alone who has extracted from me this oath: I love my country as much as I adore thy daughter; I fwear by her, and before you, that the enemies of the republic have always been, and fhall never ceafe to be mine: I fwear that I will fpill the very laft drop of my blood, to chafe thofe foreigners out of Poland, who reign there in the name of its king!

Embrace me, Lovzinfki! I now recognize you; I adopt you for my fon-in-law.—My children, all our misfortunes are at an end.

Pulaufki defired me to unite my hand to Lodoifka's, in token of our union; and we were embracing the brave palatine at the very moment that Titfikan re-entered.

Good, good! exclaims the chieftain: this is

what I wished; I am fond of marriages.—Father, I shall instantly order you to be unbound.

"By my sabre! adds the Tartar, while his followers were cutting the cords with which the hands and feet of Pulauski were tied: by my sabre! I shall do a noble action, but it will cost me a world of wealth. Two grandees of Poland! a beautiful maiden! They would have produced me a large ransom.

Titsikan, such a thought is not worthy of you! says Pulauski, interrupting him.

No! no! rejoins the Tartar, it is a mere reflection only—it is one of those ideas which a robber cannot prevent.—My brave and unfortunate friends, I demand nothing from you—nay, more, you shall not retire on foot; I have some charming horses, with which I intend to present you. And; for this lady, if you please, I will give you a litter, on which I myself have been carried for these last ten or twelve days. This young man here had given me such a wound, that I could no longer sit on horse-back. The litter is indeed a bad one, clumsily constructed, by means of branches of trees; but I have nothing except that, or a little covered waggon, to offer you, choose which ever of them you please.

In the mean time, Dourlinski, who had not as yet uttered a single word, remained with his eyes fixed upon the ground, while an air of consternation was spread over his countenance.

Unworthy friend, says Pulauski to him, how could you so cruelly abuse the confidence I reposed in you? Were you not afraid to expose yourself to my resentment? What demon blinded you?

Love, replies Dourlinski, an outrageous love! You, perhaps, do not comprehend to what excess the passions may hurry on a man, violent and jealous by nature. This frightful example, however ought to teach you, that a daughter charming as yours, is a treasure which one ought not to entrust to any person.

Pulauski, I have, indeed, merited your hatred; but I am still worthy of your pity. I have rendered myself exceedingly culpable; but you behold me cruelly punished. I lose, in one single day, my rank, my riches, my honour, my liberty! more than all this, I lose thy daughter.

O, Lodoiska, lovely maiden, whom I have so much outraged, will you deign to forget my persecutions, your danger, and your grief? Will you deign to grant to me a generous pardon?

Ah, if there are no crimes which a sincere repentance cannot expiate, Lodoiska, I am no longer criminal. I would I were able, at the price of all my blood, to redeem those tears which I have occasioned you to shed. Amidst the horrible ſtate to which Dourlinſki is about to be reduced, ſhall he not be permitted to carry with him the conſoling recollection of having heard you tell him, that he is no longer odious to you?

Too amiable, and, until this preſent moment, too unfortunate maiden, however great my wrongs may have been in regard to you, I have it in my power, to repair them all by means of a ſingle word—advance—approach me—I have a ſecret which can only be entruſted to your private ear: it is exceedingly important that it ſhould be revealed to you.

Lodoiska, without the leaſt dread, now leaves my ſide, and advances towards him without the leaſt diſtruſt.

At that very moment I beheld a poignard glittering in the hand of Dourlinſki.

I precipitate myſelf upon him.—It was too late; for I could only parry the ſecond thruſt; and the lovely Lodoiſka, wounded immediately above the left breaſt, had already fallen ſenſeleſs at the feet of Titſikan!

Pulauſki, furious at the horrid treaſon, drew his ſabre as quick as lightning, on purpoſe to avenge his daughter's fate.

No! no! exclaimed the Tartar, at the ſame time withholding his arm: you are about to make this wretch ſuffer too gentle a death!

It is well, says this infamous assassin, addressing himself to me, and at the same time, contemplating his victim with a cruel joy. Lovzinski, you appeared but now eager to be united with Lodoiska; why do you not follow her? Go, my too happy rival, go and accompany your mistress to the tomb! Let them prepare my *punishment;* it will appear pleasant to me: I leave you to torments no less cruel, and infinitely longer than mine.

Dourlinski was not allowed to utter another sentence, for the Tartars rushed in upon him, and threw him into the midst of the burning ruins.

* * * * * *
* * * * * *

What a night! my dear Faublas; how many different cares, how many opposite sentiments agitated my unhappy mind during its continuance! How many times did I experience the successive emotions of fear, hope, grief and joy. After so many dangers and inquietudes, Lodoiska was at length presented to me by her father, and I was intoxicated with the dear hope of possessing her: —a barbarian had but now assassinated her in my presence!

This was the most cruel and unfortunate moment of any during the whole course of my life!—But be comforted, my friend; my happiness, eclipsed as it were, in a single instant, was not long in shining forth with all its former splendour.

Amidst the Tartars belonging to Titsikan, was one somewhat conversant in surgery. We send for him; on his arrival he examines the wound, and assures us, that it is but a slight one. The infamous Dourlinski, constrained by his chains, and blinded by his despair, had happily been prevented from giving any other than an ill-directed blow.

As soon as Titsikan was informed that the life of Lodoiska was not in any danger, he prepared to take leave of us.

I leave you, said he, the five domestics who accompanied Pulauski; provisions for several days, arms, six excellent horses, two covered waggons, and all the people belonging to Dourlinski in chains. Their base lord is no more! Adieu! the day is about to appear; do not leave this place until to-morrow; I shall then visit the other cantons. Adieu, brave Poles! tell to your countrymen that Titsikan is not so bad as he has been represented to them, and that he sometimes restores with one hand what he takes with another. Adieu!

At these words he lifts his hand to his head, and having saluted us gracefully, after the manner of his country, he gives the signal to depart: the Tartars mount their fleet coursers in an instant, pass along the drawbridge, and make for the neighbouring plain at a full gallop.

They had been gone scarcely two hours when several of the neighbouring nobility, supported by a detachment of militia, came on purpose to invest the castle of Dourlinski.

Pulauski himself went out to receive them: he related the particulars of all that had occurred; and some, gained over by his eloquence, promised to follow us to the palatinate of Lublin.

They asked for only two days to prepare every thing necessary for the expedition, and actually came and rejoined us at the appointed time, to the number of sixty.

Lodoiska having assured us, that she was now able to undergo the fatigues of a journey, we placed her in a commodious carriage, which we had luckily been able to procure for this purpose.

After having restored Dourlinski's people to liberty, we abandon the two covered waggons to them, in which Titsikan, acting with his usual generosity, had left part of his immense booty: this we divided among them in equal proportions.

We arrived, without meeting with an accident, at Polowiski, in the palatinate of Lublin, this being the place which Pulauski had appointed for the general rendezvous.—The news of his return having gone abroad, a crowd of malecontents in the space of less than a month, flooked to and increased our little army to such a degree, that we soon found it to amount to no less than 10,000 men.

Lodoiska, entirely cured of her wound, and perfectly recovered from her fatigues, had regained her usual spirits, and appeared in possession of all her former beauty. Pulauski, one day, called me into his tent, and spoke as follows: Three thousand Russians have appeared, as you well know, upon the heights above, and at no greater distance than half a league from us; take, in the course of the ensuing night, three thousand chosen men, and go and chase the enemy from the advantageous posts which they now occupy. Recollect, that on the success of a first attempt, depends almost always that of the campaign; recollect, that you are about to avenge your country's wrongs; recollect too, my friend, that to-morrow I shall learn thy victory, and, that to-morrow also, thou shalt espouse Lodoiska?

I began my march about ten o'clock.—At midnight we surprised our enemies in their camp. Never was a defeat more complete: we killed seven hundred men; we took nine hundred prisoners; we seized all their cannon, the military chest, and the ammunition.

At break of day Pulauski marches out to join

me with the remainder of the troops: he brings Lodoiſka along with him: we are married in Pulauſki's tent. All the camp refounds with ſongs of gladneſs: valour and beauty are celebrated in joyous epithalamiums: it ſeemed to be the feſtival of Venus and Mars; and it might be truly ſaid, that every foldier appeared to be impreſſed with the fame fentiments as myſelf, and that they all partook of my happineſs.

After I had given up the firſt days of ſo dear an union entirely to love, I began to think of recompenſing the heroic fidelity of Boleſlas. My father-in-law preſented him with one of his caſtles, ſituate at ſome leagues from the capital; and Lodoiſki and myſelf added to this princely donation a confiderable fum in ready money, on purpoſe to enable him to lead an independent and tranquil life.

He firſt refuſed to leave us, but we commanded him to go and take poſſeſſion of his caſtle, and live peaceably in that honourable retreat which his fervices had ſo amply merited. On the day of his departure I took him afide:—You muſt go in my name, faid I, and wait upon our monarch at Warſaw: inform him that I am united in the bonds of Hymen to the daughter of Pulauski: ſtate to him that I am armed on purpoſe to chafe out of his kingdom thoſe foreigners who are ravaging it; and tell him, in particular, that Louvzinski, a foe to the Ruffians, is not the enemy of his king.

I will not fatigue you, my dear Faublas, with the recital of our operations, during eight fucceeding years of a bloody war.—Sometimes vanquifhed; much oftener victorious; equally great in the midft of a defeat, as formidable after a victory, and always fuperior to events, Pulauski attracted and fixed the attention of all Europe, whom he aftonifhed by his long and vigorous refiftance. Obliged to abandon one province, he made incurfions into, and performed new prodigies of valour in another: and it was thus, that in marching fucceffively throughout all the palatinates, he fignalized in each of them, by fome glorious exploit, that eternal hatred which he had fworn againft the enemies of Poland.

Wife of a warrior, daughter of a hero, accuftomed to the tumult of a camp, Lodoiska accompanied us every where. Of five children which fhe had borne me, an only daughter alone remained to us, about eighteen months old. One day, after a moft obftinate engagement, the victorious Ruffians precipitated themfelves towards my tent, on purpofe to plunder it. Pulauski and mfelf, followed by fome nobles, flew to the defence of Lodoiska, whom we faved

G

with difficulty: my daughter, however, had been carried off.

This lovely child, by a sage precaution which her mother had wisely made use of in those times of intestine commotion, had the arms of our family impressed, by means a chemical preparation, under her left breast: but my search after my daughter has hitherto been ineffectual. Alas, Dorliska, my dear Dorliska, either exists in slavery, or exists no more!

This loss affected me with the most lively sorrow; Pulauski, however, appeared, almost insensible to my misfortunes; either because his mind was occupied at this moment with the great project which he soon after communicated to me, or because the miseries of his country alone could effect his stoic heart. He, as usual, re-assembles the remains his army, takes possession of an advantageous post, employs several days in fortifying, and maintains himself in it for three whole months, against all the efforts of the Russians.

It, however, became at length necessary that he should abandon this situation, as provisions were beginning to be scarce—Pulauski, on this occasion, came to my tent; and, having ordered every one to retire, when we alone remained, he addressed me as follows:

Lovzinſki, I have juſt reaſon for complaining of your conduct. Formerly you ſupported, along with me, the burden of command, and I was enabled to divide with my ſon-in-law a part of my laborious avocations: but for theſe two laſt months, you do nothing but weep: you ſigh like a woman. You have abandoned me in a critical moment, when your aſſiſtance was become the moſt neceſſary. You ſee how I am attacked on all ſides; I fear not for myſelf; I am not unhappy for my own life: but if we periſh, the ſtate has no longer any defenders.

Awake, Lovzinſki! how nobly you once participated in my cares. Do not now remain the uſeleſs witneſs of them. We are indeed bathed in Ruſſian blood: our fellow-citizens are avenged, but they are not ſaved: nay, even in a ſhort time we may be able no longer to defend them.

You aſtoniſh me, Pulauſki! Whence theſe ſiniſter auguries?

I am not alarmed without reaſon. Conſider our preſent poſition: I am forced to awaken in every heart the love of its country; I have found no where but degenerate men, born for ſlavery, or weak ones, who, although penetrated with a ſenſe of their own misfortunes, have bounded all their views to barren complaints.

Some true citizens are, indeed, ranged under

my standards; but eight long and bloody campaigns have lessened their number, and almost extinguished them. I become enfeebled by my very victories; our enemies appear more numerous after their defeats.

I repeat to you, Pulauski, once more, that you astonish me! In circumstances no less disastrous, no less unhappy, than the present, I have beheld you sustain yourself by your courage. . . . .

Do you think that it now abandons me! True valour does not consist in being blind to danger, but in braving it after it has been foreseen. Our enemies prepare for my defeat; however, if you choose, Lovzinski, the very day which they point out for their triumph, shall perhaps be that destined to record their ruin, and atchieve the safety of our fellow-citizens.

If I choose! Can you doubt my sentiments? Speak! what would you have done?

To strike the boldest stroke that I ever meditated. Forty chosen men are assembled at Czenstachow along with Kaluvski, whose bravery is well known; they want a chief, able, firm, intrepid—It is you whom I have chosen.

Pulauski, I am ready.

I will not dissemble to you the danger of the enterprize; the event is doubtful, and, if you do not succeed, your ruin is inevitable.

I tell you that I am ready, therefore explain yourself.

You are not ignorant, that scarce four thousand men now fight under my command: with these undoubtedly I have still an opportunity of tormenting our enemies; but with such feeble means, I dare not hope to be ever able to force them to leave our provinces. All the nobility would flock beneath our banners, if the king were in my camp.

What do you say? Can you hope that the king would ever consent to repair hither?

No; but he must be forced to do so.

Forced!

Yes. I know that an ancient friendship connects you with M. de P——: but since you have supported, along with Pulauski, the cause of liberty, you know also that you ought to sacrifice every thing to the good of your country: that an interest so sacred——

I know my duty, and I am ready to fulfil it; but what is it that you now propose to me? the king never leaves Warsaw.

True; and it is, therefore, at Warsaw that you must go and find him; it is from the heart of the capital that he must be forced.

What preparations have you made for so great an enterprise?

You behold you Ruffian army, three times as ſtrong as mine, and which has been encamped three months in ſight of us: its general, tranquil at preſent within his entrenchments, impatiently waits until, forced by famine, I ſhall ſurrender myſelf at diſcretion.

Behind my camp are marſhes which he thinks impracticable: the moment that it is night, we ſhall traverſe them. I have difpoſed of every thing in ſuch a manner, that the enemy will be deceived, and not perceive my retreat until it is too late. I hope, therefore, to be able to ſteal more than an hour's march upon them, and, if fortune feconds me, perhaps a whole day. I ſhall advance ſtrait forward to Warſaw, by the great road that leads to that capital, notwithſtanding the efforts of the little Ruffian bands who hover continually in its neighbourhood. I ſhall either encounter or conquer theſe ſeparately, or, if they form a junction on purpoſe to ſtop my progreſs, I ſhall at leaſt be able to occupy their attention in ſuch a manner, that they will not be able to impede your operations.

In the mean time, Lovzinſki, you will have preceded me. Your forty followers difguiſed, and armed only with fabres, poignards and piſtols, concealed under their clothes, ſhall have arrived at Warſaw by different roads. You muſt wait there until the king has left his palace; you are then to carry him off, and to bring him to my camp. The enterprize is bold—rash, if you please so to term it: the march to Warsaw is difficult; the stay in it dangerous; the return from it extremely perilous. If you are vanquished, if you are taken prisoner, you will perish, Lovzinski, but you will perish a martyr to liberty; and Pulauski, jealous of so glorious an end, sighing at being obliged to survive you, shall send Russians, thousands of Russians, to accompany you to the tomb.

But on the contrary, if an all-powerful deity, if a god, the protector of Poland, has inspired me with this hardy object, to terminate evils; if thy good fortune shall procure a success equal to thy courage, what a glorious prosperity will be atchieved by means of this noble daring.

M. de P—— will not see, in my camp, other than citizen soldiers, the foes of foreigners, but still faithful to their king; under my patriotic tents, he will respire, as it were, the air of liberty, and the love of his country; the enemies of the state shall become his; our brave nobility, ashamed of their indolence, will readily combat under the royal banners, for the common cause; the Russians shall either be cut in pieces, or be obliged to pass the frontiers—my friend, in thee thy country shall behold her saviour. * * *

Pulauski held his word. That very night he accomplished his retreat, with equal skill and success, by traversing the marshes in profound silence. My friend, said my father-in-law to me, as soon as we were out of the reach of the enemy, it is now time that you should leave us. I know well that my daughter has more courage than another woman; but she is a tender wife, and an unfortunate mother. Her tears will affect you, and you will lose in her embraces that strength of mind, that dignity of soul, which now become more necessary to you than ever: I advise you, therefore, to be gone, without bidding her farewel.

Pulauski pressed me, but in vain, for I was unable to consent. As soon as Lodoiska knew that I should depart alone, and perceived that we were resolved not to inform her whither, she shed torrents of tears and strove to detain me. I began to hesitate.

Lovzinski, cries my father-in-law, at this critical moment, Lovzinski, depart. Wife, children, relations, all ought to be sacrificed, when it is necessary for the salvation of your country.

I instantly mount my horse, and make such haste, that I arrived by the middle of next day at Czenstachow. I here found forty brave men waiting for me, and determined for the most hazardous enterprize.

Gentlemen, said I to them, we are now met on purpose to carry a king out of the midst of his own capital. Those capable of attempting such a bold enterprize, are alone capable of effecting it: either success or death awaits us.

After this short harangue, we prepare to depart. Kaluvski, forewarned of our design, had already procured twelve waggons, loaded with hay and straw; each of which was drawn by four good horses.

We instantly disguised ourselves as peasants; we hide our clothes, our sabres, our pistols, and the saddles of our horses, in the hay with which our waggons were partly filled; we agree upon certain signs, and I give them a *watch-word*, to be used according to circumstances.—Twelve of the conspirators, commanded by Kaluvski, enter into Warsaw, accompanied by as many waggons, which they themselves conduct. I divide the rest of my little troop into several brigades, on purpose to avoid suspicion: each is ordered to march at some distance from the other, and to gain the capital by different gates.

We depart, and on Saturday the 2d of November, 1771, arrive at Warsaw, and lodge together at a convent belonging to the Dominicans.

On the next day, which was Sunday, and which will for ever form a memorable epoch in the annals of Poland, one of my people, of the name of Stravinski, being covered with rags, places himself near the collegiate church, and soon after proceeds, demanding charity even at the gates of the royal palace, where he observes every thing that passed. Several of the conspirators walked up and down the six narrow streets in the neighbourhood of the great square where Kaluvski himself was posted. We remain in ambuscade during the whole day, and part of the afternoon.

At six o'clock at night the king leaves the palace; he is followed, and is seen to enter the hotel of his uncle, the grand chancellor of Lithuania.

All our followers receive notice of this event, and assemble instantly; they throw off their miserable clothes, saddle their horses, and prepare their arms, in the large square belonging to the convent, where their movements are entirely concealed. They then sally forth, one after the other, under favour of the night. Too well known in Warsaw to hazard appearing there, without disguising myself, I still wear my peasant's dress, and I mount an excellent horse, caparisoned, however, after the common manner.

I then point out to my followers the different posts in the suburbs, which I had assigned them before our departure from the convent, and they were difperfed in fuch a manner, that all the avenues to the palace of the grand chancellor were carefully and ftrictly guarded.

Between nine and ten o'clock at night, the king comes forth on purpofe to return home; and we remark, with joy, that his attendants were far from being numerous.

The carriage was preceded by two men, who carried *flambeaux*, fome officers of his fuite, two gentlemen and an efquire followed. I know not what was the name of the grandee in the coach along with the king. There were two pages, one at each door, two hey-dukes running by the fide of the equipage, and three footmen, in the royal livery, behind.

The king proceeds flowly: part of my people affemble at fome diftance; twelve of the moft determined fpring forward: I put myfelf at their head, and we advanced at a good pace.

As there was a Ruffian garrifon at that very moment in Warfaw, we affect to fpeak the language of thofe foreigners, fo that our petty troop might be miftaken for one of their patroles.

We overtook the carriage at about a hundred and fifty paces from the grand chancellor's palace, and exactly between thofe of the bifhop of Cracow and of the late grand general of Poland.

All of a fudden we pafs the heads of the

foremost horses, so that those who preceded, found themselves separated from those who surrounded the royal equipage.

I instantly give the signal agreed upon. Kaluvski gallops up, with the remainder of the conspirators: I present a pistol to the postillion, who instantly stops; the coachman is fired upon, and is precipitated beneath the wheels. Of the two hey-dukes who endeavoured to defend their prince, one drops, pierced with two balls; the other is overturned by means of a backhanded stroke from a sabre, which he receives on the head; the steed belonging to the esquire, falls down covered with wounds: one of the pages is dismounted, and his horse taken; pistol balls fly about in all directions —in short, the attack was so hot, and the fire so violent, that I trembled for the king's life.

He himself, however, preserving the utmost coolness in the midst of the danger, had now descended from his carriage, and was striving to regain his uncle's palace on foot. Kaluvski arrests and seizes him by the hair; seven or eight of the conspirators surround, disarm, overpower him, and, pressing him between their horses, make off at full gallop, towards the end of the street.

During this moment, I confess to you, that I thought Pulauski had basely deceived me; that the death of the monarch was resolved upon, and that a plot had been formed to assassinate him.

All of a sudden I form my resolves; I clap spurs to my horse, overtake the little band, cry out to them to stop, and threaten to kill the first person who dare to disobey me.

That God who is the protector of good kings, watched over the safety of M. de P——. Kaluvski and his followers stop at the sound of my well known voice. We mount the king on horseback, make off at full speed, and regained the ditch that surrounded the city, which the monarch is constrained to leap, in company with us.

At that moment a panic terror takes possession of my troop: at fifty paces distant from the ramparts, there were no more than seven who surrounded the person of the king.

The night was dark and rainy, and it was necessary to dismount at every instant, on purpose to sound the morass with which we were surrounded.

The horse on which the monarch rode fell twice, and broke his leg at the second fall: during these violent movements, his majesty lost his *pelisse*,* and the shoe belonging to his left foot.

If you wish that I should follow you, says he to us, you must furnish me with another horse and a pair of boots.

We remount him once more, and on purpose

---
* Fur cloak.

to gain the road by which Pulauski had promised me to advance, we resolved to pass through a village called Burakow: but the king exclaims, do not go that way; there are Russians there!

I immediately change our *route;* but in proportion as we advance through the wood of Beliany, our number continue to diminish. In a short time I perceive nobody around me but Kaluvski and Stravinski; a few minutes after we are challenged by a Russian centinel on horseback, at whose voice we instantly stop, greatly alarmed for our safety.

Let us kill him, cries the ferocious Kaluvski, pointing to the king. I instantly avow to him, without disguise, the horror which such a proposition inspired me with. Very well, you may then take upon you the task of conducting him, adds this cruel hearted man, who immediately after precipitates himself into the woods. Stravinski follows him, and I alone remain with the king.

Lovzinski, says he, addressing himself to me, as soon as they were out of sight; it is you, I can no longer doubt it; it is you, for I well remember your voice. I utter not a single word in reply. He then mildly adds, it is certainly you, Lovzinski. Who would have thought this ten years ago?

We find ourselves at that moment near to the convent of Beliany, distant no more than a single league from Warsaw.

Lovzinski, continues the king, permit me to enter this convent, and save yourself.

You must follow me, was my only answer.

It is in vain, rejoins the monarch, that you are disguised; it is in vain that you endeavour to assume a feigned voice: I know you well; I am fully assured that you are Lovzinski:—ah, who would have said so ten years since? you would then have lost your life, on condition of preserving that of your friend.

His majesty now ceases to speak; we advance some time, in a profound silence, which he again breaking, exclaims, I am overcome with fatigue—*If you wish to carry me alive, permit me to repose myself for a single moment.*

I assist him to descend from his horse; he sits down upon the grass, and making me sit down by his side, he takes one of my hands and presses it between his own:

Lovzinski, you whom I have so much loved, you who know better than any one the purity of my intentions, how comes it about that you have taken up arms against me. Ungrateful Lovzinski, shall I never find you but amongst my most bitter enemies; do you return but on purpose to sacrifice me.

He then, in the most affecting language, recapitulates the pleasures of our early youth; our more intimate connection at an age approaching to manhood, the tender friendship which we had sworn to each other, and the regard which he had ever treated me with since that period. He spoke to me of the honours with which he would have loaded me during his reign, if I had been ambitious to merit them: he reproached me more particularly, respecting the unworthy enterprize of which I appeared to be the leader, but of which, he said, he was well assured, that I was no more than the instrument.

He threw all the horror of the plot upon Pulauski, representing to me, at the same time, that the author of such an attempt was not the less culpable person; that I could not charge myself with its execution, without committing a crime; and that this odious complaisance, so highly treasonable in a subject, was infinitely more so in a friend. He concluded, by pressing me to restore him to his liberty: fly, said he to me, and be assured, if I encounter any of the Russian parties, I shall tell them that you have taken an opposite road from that which you have taken

The king continued to press me with the most earnest entreaties: his natural eloquence, augmented by the danger of his situation, carried persuasion to my heart, and awakened the most tender sentiments there.

I confefs that I was ftaggered; I balanced the circumftances for fome time in my own mind, but Pulauski at length triumphed.

I thought that I ftill heard the fierce republican reproaching me with my pufillanimity. My dear Faublas, the love of one's country has, perhaps its fanaticifm and its fuperftitions: but if I was then culpable, I am ftill fo; I am more than ever purfuaded, that in obliging the king to remount his horfe again, I performed an action that reflected honour on my patriotifm.

Is it thus, fays he to me, in a melancholy accent, that you reject the prayer addreffed to you by a friend! that you refufe the pardon offered to you by your king? Well, then, let us be gone. I deliver myfelf up to my unhappy fate, or rather I abandon you to your's.

We now recommence our journey once more; but the entreaties of the monarch, his arguments, his reproaches, his very menaces, the ftruggles which I felt within myfelf, affected me in fuch a manner, that I no longer could difcern my way. Wandering up and down the country, I kept no one certain road: after half an hour's fatigue, we found ourfelves at Marimont,* and I was

---

* Marimont is a country houfe belonging to the court of Saxony; it is nearer Warfaw, by half a league than Bellany.

greatly alarmed at seeing us thus return towards Warsaw, instead of leaving it at a distance.

At about a quarter of a league beyond this, we unfortunately fell in with a party of Russians. The king immediately discovers himself to the commanding officer, and then instantly adds: In the course of the preceding afternoon, I happened to bewilder myself during the chace; this good peasant, whom you see here, insisted on my partaking a frugal repast in his cottage; but as I thought that I perceived some of the soldiers of Pulauski roaming in the neighbourhood, I was desirous of returning to Warsaw immediately, and you will oblige me much by instantly accompanying me thither.

As to you, my friend, continues he, turning at the same time towards me, I am not at all sorry that you have given yourself this uselefs trouble, for I am as much pleased at returning to my capital, attended by these gentlemen (pointing at the same time to the escort) as in accompanying you any farther. However, it would be improper that I should leave you without any recompense; what are you desirous of? Speak—I will grant you any favour which you may demand of me.

Faublas, you may easily conceive how much I was alarmed, for I was still doubtful of the king's intentions. I endeavoured therefore to discover the true meaning of his equivocal difcourfe, which muft be either full of a bitter irony, or a magnanimous addrefs. M. de P—— left me for fome time in this cruel uncertainty: I behold you greatly embarraffed, continues he at length, with a gracious air; you know not what to choofe! Come then, my friend, embrace me: there is indeed more honour than profit in embracing a king (adds he with a fmile); however, it muft be allowed, that in my place, many monarchs would not be at this moment fo generous as myfelf! On uttering thefe words, he inftantly departs, leaving me penetrated with gratitude, and confounded with fo much true greatnefs.

However, the danger which the king had fo generoufly relieved me from, began every moment to affail me again. It was more than probable that a great number of couriers expedited from Warfaw, had fpread about on all fides the aftonifhing news of the king's having been carried off. Already, without doubt, the ravifhers were warmly purfued. My remarkable drefs might betray me in my flight; and if I once more fell into the hands of any of the Ruffians, better informed of the circumftance, all the efforts of the king would not be able to fave me. Suppofing Pulauski had obtained all the fuccefs which he expected, he muft ftill be at a great diftance; a journey of ten more leagues at least remained for me to perform, and my horse was entirely spent with fatigue; I endeavoured, however, to spur him on, but he had not got five hundred paces before he fell under me.

A cavalier, well mounted, happened to pass along the road by the side of me, at this very moment: he perceived the poor animal tumble down, and, thinking to amuse himself at the expense of an unfortunate peasant, he began to banter me about my situation.—Piqued at this buffoonry, I resolved to punish him for his raillery, and secure my own flight at one and the same time: I therefore instantly present one of my pistols to his breast, and oblige him to surrender his own horse to me; nay, I acknowledge to you, that, forced by the peculiarity of my situation, I despoiled him even of his cloak, which being very large, hid all my rags beneath it, which otherwise might have discovered me. I then cast my purse full of gold at the feet of the astonished traveller, and sprang forward as fast as my new horse could carry me.

Luckily for me, he was fresh and vigorous. I dart forward twelve leagues, with all the swiftness of an arrow: at length I think I hear the firing of cannon, and I instantly conjecture that my father-in-law was at hand, and was employed in fighting the Russians.

I was not deceived—I arrive on the field of battle at the very moment when one of our regiments had given way. I inftantly difcovered myfelf to the fugitives, and having rallied them beneath a neighbouring hill, I attack the enemies in flank, while Pulauski charges them in front with the remainder of his troops. Our manœuvres were fo well concerted, and fo admirably executed, that the Ruffians were entirely routed, after experiencing a terrible carnage.

Pulauski deigned to attribute to me the honour of their defeat: Ah! cries he, embracing me, after hearing the particulars of my expedition—ah! if your forty followers had but equalled you in courage, the king would have been at this very moment in my camp! But the Deity does not will it. I am grateful, however, that you have been preferved to us; and I return you thanks for the important fervice which you have rendered me: but for you, Kaluvski would have affaffinated the monarch, and my name would have been covered with an eternal opprobrium!

I might have been able, added he, to have advanced two miles farther; but I rather chofe to take poffeffion of this refpectable poft, on account of the fecurity of my camp. Yefterday, in the courfe of my march, I furprifed, and cut in pieces, a party of Ruffians; this morning I beat two more of their detachments; but another confiderable corps having collected the remainder of the vanquifhed, took advantage of the darknefs of the night, on purpofe to attack me. My foldiers, fatigued with the toil of a long march, and three fucceeding engagements, began to fly; but victory returned to my camp at your approach. Let us entrench ourfelves here; we will wait for the Ruffian army, and fight while we yet have a drop of blood remaining.

In the mean time, the camp refounded with the cries of gladnefs, and our victorious foldiers mingled my praifes with thofe of Pulaufki. At the noife of my name, repeated by a thoufand tongues, Lodoifka ran to her father's tent. She convinced me of the excefs of her tendernefs, by the excefs of her joy at our meeting; and I was obliged once more to commence the recital of the dangers from which I had efcaped. She could not hear of the fingular generofity of the monarch, when I was in the power of the Ruffians, without fhedding tears: how magnanimous he is, exclaims fhe, amidft a tranfport of joy; how worthy of being a king, he who fo generoufly pardoned you! How many fighs has he fpared a wife whom you forfake! how many tears the loving wife whom you are not afraid of facrificing! Cruel Lovzinski, are not the dangers to which you daily expofe yourfelf fufficient——

Pulauski here interrupts his daughter with a certain degree of harshness: Indiscreet and weak woman! exclaims he, is it before me that you dare to hold such a discourse as this?

Alas! replies she in a mild accent, alas! must I forever tremble for the life of a father and a husband! Lodoiska also made the most affecting complaints to me, and sighed after a more happy futurity, while fortune was preparing for us the most cruel reverse.

Our Cossacks, placed at the out-posts, now came in from all parts, and informed us that the Russian army was approaching. Pulauski reckoned on being attacked at break of day; but he was not: however, about the middle of the following night, I was informed that the enemy was preparing to force our entrenchments.

Pulauski, always ready, always active, was actually defending them: during the course of this fatal night, he atchieved every thing that might have been expected from his valour and experience.

We repel the assailants no less than five different times; but they return unceasingly to the charge, pour in fresh troops at every new attack, and, during the last one, penetrate into the heart of our very camp by three different avenues, and at one and the same time.

Zaremba was killed by my fide; a crowd of nobles fell in this bloody action; the enemy refufed to give any quarter. Furious at feeing all my friends perifh before my eyes, I refolved to precipitate myfelf into the midft of the Ruffian battalions.

Heedlefs man! exclaims Pulauski, what blind fury urges you towards your deftruction? My army is entirely routed—deftroyed —but my courage ftill remains! Why fhould we perifh ufelefs here ? Let us begone! I will conduct you into climes where we may raife up new enemies againft the Ruffian name. Let us live, fince we can ftill ferve our country! Let us fave ourfelves let us fave Lodoiska!

Lodoiska! am I capable of abandoning her?

We inftantly run to her tent—we are fcarce in time: we carry her off; precipitate ourfelves into the neighbouring woods, and on the next morning we venture to fally forth, and prefent ourfelves before the gate of a caftle that was not altogether unknown to us.

It indeed belonged to a noble Pole, who had ferved during fome time in our army. Miciflas inftantly comes forth, and offers an afylum, which he advifes us, however, to make ufe of for a few hours only. He informs us, that a very aftonifhing piece of news had fpread abroad on the former evening, and began to be confirmed, according to which the king himself had been carried away out of Warsaw; that the Russians had pursued the conspirators, and brought back the monarch to his capital; and that, in fine, it was talked of putting a price upon the head of Pulauski, who was suspected of being the author of this treason.

Believe me, says he, when I assure you, whether you have engaged or not in this bold plot, that you ought to fly; leave your uniforms here, which will assuredly betray you: I will instantly supply you with clothes which are less remarkable; and as to Lodoiska, I myself will conduct her to the place which you have chosen for your retreat.

Lodoiska now interrupts Micislas: the place of my retreat shall be that of their flight, for I will accompany them every where.

Pulauski represents to his daughter, that she was not able to sustain the fatigue incident to such a long journey, and that besides we should be liable to continual dangers.

The greater the peril is, replies she, the more I ought to partake it with you. You have repeated to me a hundred times, that the daughter of Pulauski ought not to be an ordinary woman. For the last eight years I have constantly lived in the midst of alarms; I have seen nothing but scenes of carnage and horror. Death has environed me on all sides, and menaced me at every moment: will you not permit me to brave it now by your side? Is not the life of Lodoiska connected with that of her father? Lovzinski, will not the stroke that fells you to the ground send your wife to the grave? and am I no longer worthy——

I now interrupt Lodoiska, and join with her father, in stating the reasons which determined us to leave her in Poland.—She hears me with impatience: Ungrateful man, exclaims she at length, will you fly without me? You shall remain, replies Pulauski, with Lovzinski's sisters, and I prohibit you.

His daughter, now frantic with grief, would not permit him to finish the sentence

I know your rights, my father! I respect them; they shall always appear sacred to me: but you do not possess that of separating a wife from her husband.

Ah, pardon me! I see that I offend you—my reason no longer maintains its empire.

But pity my grief—

Excuse my despair—

My father! Lovzinski! hear me, both of you; I am determined to accompany you every where!

Yes, I will follow you every where, cruel men; I will follow you in spite of yourselves!

Lovzinski, if your wife has lost all the rights she had over your heart, recollect at least, her who was once the mistress of your affections.

Recal to your remembrance that frightful night, when I was about to perish in the flames; that terrible moment when you ascended the burning tower, crying out, let me live or die with Lodoiska

That which you felt at that terrible moment, I now experience! I know no greater evil than that of being separated from you; I now exclaim in my turn, let me either live or die with my father and my husband.

Unfortunate wretch! what will become of me, if you should forsake me. Reduced to the cruel situation of bewailing you both, where shall I find a solace for my miseries? Will my children console me?—Alas! in two years death hath snatched four away from me; and the Ruffians, equally pitiless as death itself, have bereaved me of the last. have only you remaining in the world, and even you wish to abandon me! my f**** my husband! Will such dear connections as these be insensible to my sufferings! Have compassion, take pity on your own Lodoiska!

*　*　*　*　*　*　*　*

Her tears now intercepted her speech. Miciflas wept; my heart was torn with anguish. You are resolved to accompany us, my daughter—be it so; I consent, says Pulauski: but I wish that heaven may not punish me for my complaisance!

Lodoiska now embraces us both with as much joy as if all our ills had been at an end. I leave two letters with Miciflas, which he undertook to transmit according to the direction; the one was addressed to my sisters, and the other to Boleflas. I bade him adieu, and I recommended to them, to neglect no means to endeavour to recover my dear Dorliska!

It was necessary that I should disguise my wife —she assumes a masculine dress; we change our own, and we employ all the means in our power to disfigure ourselves in such a manner as to elude research, and prevent discovery.

Thus altered in our appearance, armed with our sabres and our pistols, provided with a considerable sum in gold, with some trinkets, and all the jewels of Lodoiska, we take leave of Miciflas, and make haste to regain the woods.

Pulauski now communicates to us the design which he had formed of taking refuge in Turkey. He hoped to be employed in a situation equal to his rank and his abilities, in the armies of the grand signior, who had, for the two last years, with some difficulty, sustained a disastrous war against the Russians.

Lodoiska did not appear in the least affrighted at the long journey which we had to make; and as she could neither be known nor sought after, she insisted upon going out to reconnoitre the adjacent country, and at the same time charged herself with the fatiguing but important task of bringing us the provisions which we stood in need of.

As soon as the day appeared, we retired into the woods; hid either in the trunks of trees, or in the thick groves of pines, we waited impatiently for the return of night, on purpose to continue our march. It was thus, that, during several weeks, we were enabled to escape from the search of a multitude of different bodies of Russian troops, who were sent out on purpose to discover us, and who pursued us like so many blood hounds, animated with the passions of hatred and revenge.

One day as Lodoiska, still disguised as a peasant, was returning from a neighbouring hamlet, where she had gone on purpose to purchase the provisions which she was now conveying to us, two Russian marauders attacked her at the entry of the forest in which we were concealed.

After having robbed, they prepared to strip her. At the shrieks which she uttered, we hastened from our retreat, and the two ruffians immediately betake themfelves to flight upon our appearance: but we were greatly alarmed left they fhould recount this adventure to their companions, whofe fufpicions, aroufed by this fingular rencounter, might induce them to come and drag us from our afylum.

After a moft fatiguing journey, we entered Polefia.* Pulauski wept at leaving his native country.

At leaft, exclaims he, with a mournful accent—at leaft I have faithfully ferved you, and I now only go into exile, that I may be enabled to ferve you again.

So many fatigues had exhaufted the ftrength of Lodoiska. Arrived at Novogorod,† we refolved to ftop there on purpofe to give her time to recover her ftrength. It was our defign to remain for fome days, but fome of the country people whom we queftioned, frankly informed us, that a number of troops were in motion, in that neighbourhood, on purpofe to arreft a certain perfon of

---

* Polefia is a name given to the palatinate of Brefte, in Lithuania; Brefte, Briefcia, or Breffici, is fituated upon the banks of the river Bog.

† There are feveral towns of this name in Ruffia. This feems to have been Novogorod Welicki, or Great Novogorod, the capital of a duchy of the fame name.

the name of Pulauski, who had occafioned the king of Poland to be taken prifoner, and carried off from the midſt of his own capital.

Juſtly alarmed at this intelligence, we remain but a few hours in this town, where we, however, found means to purchafe fome horfes without being difcovered.

We then paſſed the Defna, above Czernicove;* and following the banks of the Sula, we crofs that river at Perevoloczna, where we learn, that Pulaufki, who had been traced to Novogorod, had efcaped, as it were, by miracle, and that the Ruffian foldiers, indefatigable in their purfuit, were ſtill fearching after him, and were in hopes of making him prifoner.

It was now again become neceffary to fly once more, and once more to change our route; we therefore inſtantly made for the immenfe forefts which cover the face of the country between the Sula and the Zem, in the dark retreats of which we hoped to find fhelter from our foes.

We at length difcover a cavern, in which we were reduced to the neceffity of taking up our abode. A fhe-bear difputes with us the entrance

---

* Czernicove, or Czernikou, is a confiderable town, and is the capital of the duchy of the fame name. It is fituate on the river Defna, 75 miles north-eaſt of Kiow.

into this asylum, equally solitary and frightful : we assail, we kill her, and devour her young.

Pulauski was wounded in this encounter : Lodoiska, worn out with fatigue and distress, was scarcely able to support her existence: the winter was approaching, and the cold was already excessive.

Pursued by the Russians in the inhabited parts; menaced by wild and ferocious animals in this vast desert : destitute of any arms but our swords; reduced in a short time to eat our very horses; what was to become of us?

The danger of the situation to which my father-in-law and my wife were reduced, had become so pressing, that no other fear any longer alarmed me. My personal safety, hitherto so dear to me, did not now suggest itself once to my mind: I felt only for their's. I resolved, therefore, to procure for them at any rate, those succours which their situation required, which was still more deplorable than my own; and leaving them both with the promise of rejoining them in a short time, I take a few of the diamonds belonging to Lodoiska, and follow the stream of the Warsklo.

You must know, my dear Faublas, that a traveller, bewildered amidst those vast countries, and reduced to the necessity of wandering about without a compass, and without a guide, is obliged to follow the courfe of a river, becaufe it is upon its banks that the habitations of mankind are moft commonly to be met with.

It was neceffary that I fhould gain, as foon as poffible, fome confiderable town in which a few merchants refided: I therefore journeyed along the banks of the Warfklo, and travelling day and night, found myfelf at Pultava* at the end of four days. During my refidence in this place, I pafs for a trader belonging to Bielgorod. I there learn that the Ruffian troops were ftill roaming about in purfuit of Pulauski, and that the emprefs had fent an exact defcription of his perfon every where, with orders to feize him either dead or alive, wherever he might be found.

I make hafte to fell my diamonds, to purchafe powder, arms, and provifions of all kinds, different utenfils, and fome coarfe but neceffary furniture; every thing, in fine, which I judged moft proper to relieve our mifery, and foften our misfortunes. With thefe I load a waggon, drawn by four good horfes, of which I was the only conductor.

My return was equally tedious and difficult;

* Pultoway, Pultowa, or Pultava, is a fortified town in the Ukraine, famous for a battle fought in its neighbourhood between Charles XII. of Sweden, and Peter the Great of Ruffia. It is 100 miles fouth-weft of Bielgorod, from which Lovzinfki pretended to have come on purpofe to purchafe merchandize, &c.

no lefs than eight whole days expired before I arrived at the entrance of the foreft.

It was there that terminating my difagreeable and dangerous journey, I was about to fuccour my father-in-law and my wife; and I was about to revifit all that was moft dear to me in the world; and yet my dear Faublas, I felt none of thofe tranfports of joy which fuch an event feemed likely to infpire.

Your philofophers have no belief in forebodings.

I affure you, however, my dear friend, that I experienced an involuntary uneafinefs: my mind became difpirited, difmayed, and fomething, I know not what, feemed to whifper to me, that the moft unhappy moment of my whole life was faft approaching.

On my departure I had placed feveral flint ftones at certain diftances, on purpofe to enable me to retrace my road; but I could not now difcover them. I had alfo cut off with my fabre large pieces of the bark of feveral trees, which I could not now perceive: I enter the foreft, however: I holla with all my ftrength: I difcharge my gun from time to time, but nobody anfwers me. I dared not truft myfelf among the trees and fhrubs for fear of lofing my way back; neither could I wander too far from my waggon, which was ftored with provifions fo neceffary to Pulauski, his daughter, and myfelf.

The night, which now approached, obliged me to give over my fearch, and I pafs it in the fame manner as the former. Rolled up in my cloak, I lay down beneath my waggon, which I had carefully furrounded with my larger movables, and which thus ferved me as a rampart againft the wild beafts.

I could not fleep; the cold was extremely intenfe; the fnow fell in great abundance: at break of day I looked around, and found all the ground covered with it. From that moment I formed the moft horrible and the moft finifter prefages: the ftones, which might have pointed out the path I was to have taken, were all buried, and it appeared impoffible that I fhould ever be able to difcover my father-in-law and my wife.

Had the horfe, which I left with them at my departure, afforded them fufficient fuftenance ever fince? Had not hunger, cruel hunger, obliged them to fly from their retreat? Were they ftill concealed in thofe frightful deferts? If they were not there, where fhould I be able to find them? Where, without them, fhould I drag out my miferable exiftence? * * *
* * * * * *
* * * * * *

But could I believe that Pulauski had abandoned his son-in-law? that Lodoiska had confented to feparate herfelf from her hufband? No—undoubtedly not. They were ftill confined within the circle of this frightful folitude; and if I abandoned them, they muft die with famine and with cold! * * * * *
* * * * * *
* * * * * * *

Thefe defperate reflections at length determined my conduct, and I no longer examined whether or not in removing at a diftance from my waggon, I was in danger of never finding it again. To carry fome provifions to my father-in-law and wife, to fuccour Pulauski and Lodoiska—thefe were now the only fentiments that occupied my mind.

I accordingly feize my fowling-piece, take fome powder and fhot, and load one of my horfes with neceffaries: I pierce into the woods, much farther than during the former evening. I again holla with all my ftrength; I again make frequent difcharges with my gun. The moft melancholy filence reigned all around me.

I now find myfelf in a part of the foreft where the trees were fo extremely thick, that there was no longer any paffage for my horfe: I, therefore tie him to a tree, and my defpair getting the better of every other confideration, I ftill continue to advance with my gun and part of my provifions. I had now wandered about for two hours more, my inquietude forcing me every moment to double my pace, when at length I perceive human footfteps imprinted upon the fnow.

Hope gives me new ftrength, and I therefore inftantly follow the traces which were ftill frefh. Soon after I difcovered Pulauski almoft naked, emaciated with hunger, and fo changed as fcarce to be known even by me!

He makes all the efforts in his power to drag his limbs towards me, and to reply to my enquiries. The moment that I had rejoined him, he feizes, with avidity, on the victuals that I prefented to him, and devours them in an inftant. I then demand of him where Lodoiska is.

Alas! fays he, you will fee her there! The tone of voice in which he pronounced thefe words, made me tremble. I run to, I arrive at, the cavern, but too well prepared for the melancholy fpectacle that awaited me. Lodoiska, wrapped up in her own clothes, and covered with thofe of her father, was extended upon a bed of half rotten leaves!

She raifes, with fome difficulty, her weary head, and refufing the aliments which I now offer her, addreffes me as follows:—I am not hungry!

K

The death of my children; the loss of Dorliska; our journies, so long, so laborious, so difficult: your dangers, which seemed to increase daily—these have killed me! I was unable to resist fatigue and sorrow. My friend, I am dying—I heard thy voice, and my soul was stopped in its flight—We shall meet again! Lodoiska ought to die in the arms of a husband whom she adores!—Assist my father! May he live! Live both of you—console yourselves, and forget me! * *
* * * * * * *
—Search every where for my dear * *
* * * * * *

She was unable to pronounce the name of her daughter, and instantly expired! * *
* * * * * *

Her father digs a grave for her at a little distance from the cavern; and I behold the earth inclose all that I loved in this world!
* * * * * *

What a trying moment! Pulauski alone prevented me from becoming the victim of despair: he forces me to survive Lodoiska! *
* * * * * *

Lovzinski now endeavours to continue his narrative, but his tears prevent his utterance. He demands leave to retire for a moment, passes into a neighbouring apartment, and returns in a short time after with a miniature in his hand.

Behold, says he, the portrait of my dear Dorliski! behold how handsome she was while an infant! In her features, as yet scarcely developed, I recognize those of her mother——Ah! if at length——

I now interrupt Lovzinski: What a beautiful face! exclaims I: she greatly resembles my *handsome cousin*!

These are the rhapsodies of a lover, replies he; he sees the object of his adoration every where!

Ah, my dear friend, if Dorliska were restored to me!—But after ten years of an useless search, I can no longer hope to see her again.

With his eyes still diffused with tears, which he strives to retain, Lovzinski resumes the history of his misfortunes, in a voice overcome as it were with their excess:

Pulauski, whose courage never abandoned him, and whose strength was by this time restored, obliges me to occupy myself jointly with him, in the business of procuring our subsistence.

By following along the snow the prints of my footsteps, we arrive at length at the place where I had left my waggon, which we immediately unload, and burn soon after, on purpose to withhold from our enemies the most distant suspicion of the place of our retreat.

By the aid of our horses, for which we procure

a paſſage by making a circuitous journey, inſtead of attempting to bring them ſtraight to the place of our retreat, we were at length able to tranſport thoſe proviſions and moveables to our cavern, which it was ſo neceſſary for us to procure, and to huſband, if we reſolved to remain much longer in this ſolitude. We ſoon after killed our horſes, which we were unable to ſupply with food. We lived upon their fleſh, which the rigour of the ſeaſon preſerved for a conſiderable time; it corrupted, however, at length; and our fire-arms being unable to procure us any other than a ſcanty ſupply of game, we were obliged to have recourſe to our proviſions; which, at the end of three months, were entirely conſumed.

Some gold, and the greater part of Lodoiska's diamonds, ſtill remained. Should I make a ſecond voyage to Pultava? or ſhould we both run the hazard of ſuch an undertaking, and quit our retreat in company? We had already ſuffered ſo much, and ſo cruelly in this foreſt, that we reſolved to embrace the latter reſolution.

We accordingly ſally forth; we paſs the Sem near Rylks; we purchaſe a boat there, and, diſguiſing ourſelves in the dreſs of fiſhermen, we deſcend that river, and enter the Deſna.

Our boat was viſited at Czernicove, but miſery had ſo disfigured Pulauſki, that it was impoſſible any longer to recognize him. We then enter the Dnieper; we cross from Kiof* to Krylow. There we were obliged to receive into our boat, and carry to the other side, several Russian soldiers, who were on their march to join a small army employed against Pugatchew.

At Zaporiskaia, we heard of the capture of Bender and Oczakow, the conquest of the Crimea, the defeat and subsequent death of the vizar Oglou.

Pulauski, reduced to a state of desperation, was anxious to traverse the vast deserts that separated him from Pugatchew, on purpose to join himself to that enemy of the Russians; but the excess of our fatigues obliged us to remain at Zaporiskaia.

The peace which was soon after concluded between Russia and the Porte, at length afforded us the means of entering Turkey.

On foot, and still disguised, we crossed the Boudziac, part of Moldavia, and Wallachia, and after a thousand unforeseen and unexpected difficulties and fatigues, we at length arrive at Adrianople.

---

* Kiof, or Kiow, is a palatinate, in which is situated a town of the same name, which is reckoned the capital of the Ukraine. It is built on the banks of the river Nieper, or Dnieper, as it is sometimes called.

Having remained for some time at this place, on purpose to repair our exhausted forces, we prepare to depart: but we are arrested, and, being carried before the cadi, are accused of having sold several diamonds in the course of our journey, which we had apparently stolen. The miserable clothes with which we were covered, had given rise to this suspicion.

Pulauski discovers himself to the mussulman judge, and he sends us immediately to Constantinople.

We are admitted shortly after to an audience of the grand seignior. He orders apartments to be prepared for us, and assigns us a liberal pension upon his treasury.

I then write to my sisters, and to Boleslas: we learn, by their answers, that all the property of Pulauski had been confiscated; that he was degraded from his rank, and condemned to lose his head.

My father-in-law is in the utmost consternation on receiving this inteliigence: he is filled with indignation at being accused as a regicide: he writes home in his own justification.

Constantly animated, and devoured as it were with the love of his country, continually influenced by the mortal hatred which he had sworn against its enemies, he never ceased, during the four whole years that we remained in Turkey, to endeavour, by his intrigues, to oblige the Porte to declare war againſt Ruſſia.

In 1774, amidſt a tranſport of rage, he receives intelligence of the triple invaſion,* which bereaved the republic of one-third of its poſſeſſions.

It was in the ſpring of 1776, that the inſurgents in America, fearful of the tyranny of an iſland which once boaſted of its own liberties, reſolved to redeem their violated rights by force of arms. My country hath loſt her freedom, ſays Pulauſki to me one day: but, ah, let us ſtill fight for that of a new people!

We paſs into Spain, we embark on board of a veſſel bound for the Havannah, from whence we repair to Philadelphia. The congreſs inſtantly preſents us with commiſſions, and employs us in the army of general Waſhington.

Pulauſki, conſumed with a black melancholy, expoſes his life like a man, to whom life had become inſupportable, is always to be found at the moſt dangerous poſts, and towards the end of the fourth campaign, is mortally wounded by

* The diſmemberment of Poland, by the empreſs of Ruſſia, the emperor of Germany, and the king of Pruſſia. This event which took place by the agreement of three royal robbers, is one of the moſt diſgraceful actions that ever ſtained the page of humanity.

my fide. Being carried to his tent, I inftantly repair thither to confole him.

I find that my end approaches, fays he, addreffing himfelf to me. Ah! it is but too true, that I fhall never fee my native country again!

Cruel, fantaftical deftiny! Pulaufki falls a martyr to American liberty, and the Poles ftill continue flaves! * * * *
* * * * * * *

My friend, my death would be indeed horrible, if a ray of hope did not remain to cheer me! Ah! I hope I do not deceive myfelf—No, I am not miftaken, adds he in a firmer accent.

A confoling deity difclofes in my laft thoughts a futurity, a happier futurity which approaches!

I behold one of the firft nations in the world awakening from a long and deep flumber, and re-demanding of its proud oppreffors, its violated honours, and its ancient rights; its facred, imprefcriptible rights, the rights of humanity.

I behold, in an immenfe capital, long difhonoured by every fpecies of fervility, a crowd of foldiers difcovering themfelves to be citizens, and millions of citizens becoming foldiers.

Beneath their redoubled blows, the baftile fhall be overturned; the fignal is already given from one extremity of the empire to another;—the reign of tyrants is no more!

A neighbouring people, fometimes an enemy, but always generous, always worthy of deciding upon great actions, fhall applaud thofe unexpected efforts, crowned with fuch a fpeedy fuccefs!

Ah, may a reciprocal efteem, commence, and ftrengthen between thefe two nations an unalterable friendfhip! May that horrible fcience of trick, impofture, and treafon, which courts denominate *politics*, hold out no obftacle to prevent this fraternal re-union!

Noble rivals, in talents and philofophy, Frenchmen! Englifhmen! fufpend at length, and fufpend forever, thofe bloody difcords, the fury of which has but too often extended over the two hemifpheres;—no longer decide between you the empire of the univerfe, but by the force of your example, and the afcendancy of your genius. Inftead of the cruel advantage of affrighting and fubduing the nations around you, difpute between yourfelves the more folid glory of enlightening their ignorance, and breaking their chains.

Approach, adds Pulauski; behold at a little diftance from, and in the midft of the carnage that furrounds us, among fuch a croud of famous warriors, a warrior celebrated even in the midft of them, by his mafculine courage, his early talents, and his virtues truly republican. He is the heir of a name long illuftrious; but he had no occafion for the glory of his anceftors, to render himfelf celebrated.

It is young Fayette, already an honour to France, and a fcourge to tyrants: but he has fcarce begun his immortal labours! Envy his fate, Lovzinski; endeavour to imitate his virtues, and follow as near as poffible the fteps of fo great a man. He, the worthy pupil of a Wafhington, fhall foon be the Wafhington of his own country. It is almoft at the fame time, my friend, it is at that memorable epoch of the regeneration of nations, that the eternal juftice fhall alfo prefent to our fellow-citizens, the days of vengeance and of liberty.

Then, Lovzinski, in whatever place thou mayeft be, let thy hate re-kindle Again combat glorioufly on the fide of Poland.

Let the remembrance of our injuries, and of our fucceffes, call forth thy courage: May thy fword, fo many times empurpled with the blood of our enemies, be ftill turned againft thofe oppreffors. May they tremble while thinking on thy exploits! May they tremble in recalling the name of Pulauski!

They have ravifhed from us our property; they have affaffinated thy wife; they have robbed thee of thy daughter; they have difhonoured my memory!

The barbarians! They have difmembered our provinces Lovzinski, thefe are injuries which you ought never to forget.

When our perfecutors are thofe alfo of our country, vengeance becomes at once facred and indifpenfable

You owe to the Ruffians an eternal hatred! You owe to Poland the laft drop of your blood! Saying this, he expires.*

Death, in fnatching him from me, bereaved me of my laft confolation.

My friend, I fought for the United States of America, until the happy peace which infured their independence. M. de C—— who had ferved along with me, and who was attached to the *corps* commanded by the marquis de la Fayette —M. de C—— gave me a letter of recommendation to the baron de Faublas. Your father took fuch a lively intereft in my fate, that in a very fhort time we were connected together by the bonds of the ftricteft friendfhip.

I only quitted the province in which he refided, on purpofe to come and live in Paris, where I knew that he would not be long in following me.

In the mean time, my fifters have collected the f.emall remainder of a fortune formerly immen

---

* Pulaufki was killed at the fiege of Savannah, in 1779.

Inftructed of my arrival here, and of the name which I have affumed, they have informed me, that they intend to repair to this capital, on purpofe to confole the unfortunate Duportail with their prefence.

Here ends M. Duportail's narrative. Our readers will have partly anticipated the fequel of the ftory. In the accomplifhed Sophia de Pontis, the *ci-devant* baron de Lovzinski finds his daughter, the long loft Dorliska, but not till after fhe had been feduced and carried off from the convent by young Faublas.—A reconciliation at laft takes place. Faublas is united to his Sophia. Lovzinski returns to his native country, and is reftored to his fortune, his honours, and to the favour of his fovereign.

www.ingramcontent.com/pod-product-compliance
Lightning Source LLC
Chambersburg PA
CBHW022142160426
43197CB00009B/1394